THINK
LIKE
JESUS

*What Do I Believe and
Why Does It Matter?*

STUDY GUIDE | EIGHT SESSIONS

RANDY FRAZEE

ZONDERVAN™

ZONDERVAN

Think Like Jesus Study Guide
Copyright © 2020 by Randy Frazee

This title is also available as a Zondervan ebook.

Requests for information should be addressed to: Zondervan, 3900 Sparks Dr. SE, Grand Rapids, Michigan 49546

All Scripture quotations are from The Holy Bible, New International Version®, NIV®. Copyright © 1973, 1978, 1984, 2011 by Biblica, Inc.® Used by permission. All rights reserved worldwide.

Any Internet addresses (websites, blogs, etc.) and telephone numbers in this book are offered as a resource. They are not intended in any way to be or imply an endorsement by Zondervan, nor does Zondervan vouch for the content of these sites and numbers for the life of this book.

Portions of this guide were adapted from the *Believe Study Guide* (9780310826118) and from *Think, Act, Be Like Jesus* (9780310250173) by Randy Frazee.

All rights reserved. No part of this publication may be reproduced, stored in a retrieval system, or transmitted in any form or by any means — electronic, mechanical, photocopy, recording, or any other — except for brief quotations in printed reviews, without the prior permission of the publisher.

ISBN 978-0-310-11853-4 (softcover)
ISBN 978-0-310-11854-1 (ebook)

First printing April 2020 / Printed in the United States of America

CONTENTS

HOW TO USE THIS GUIDE

Scope and Sequence

The goal of every follower of Jesus Christ is to become more like him, but how do you know where to start? What does it really mean to be a disciple of Jesus? The objective of *Think Like Jesus*—the first in a series of three small-group studies— is to start the process toward renewing your mind so that your thoughts will more closely match the thoughts of Christ. This study guide (and the related video) will help you assess your spiritual life, pinpoint areas that need special attention, and give you tools to help you grow. The eight sessions in this study will focus on the core beliefs of the Christian faith. The next study in this series, *Act Like Jesus*, will focus on foundational practices of the Christian life. The final study, *Be Like Jesus*, will focus on Christlike virtues. May God bless you as you seek him through this experience!

Session Outline

Each session is divided into two parts. In the group section, you and your group will begin by watching a short video teaching from Randy Frazee and follow along with the note-taking outline that has been provided. You will then recite the key verse, the key idea, and engage in some guided group discussion through the questions provided. At the end of the group time, you will be given real-life scenarios of people who struggle with their faith. Using the key applications from your study guide, your group will be challenged to think of ways to encourage the people within these case studies. Finally, you will close the group with a time of prayer.

Personal Study

At the end of the group section, you will find a series of readings and study questions for you to go through on your own during the week. Each of these sections will challenge you to consider a key question about the topic, think through a key idea, and then consider a key application regarding the difference it should make in your life. You will also be given four statements to help you evaluate the alignment of your life with the key idea and asked to take action by memorizing each session's key idea and key verse. **The personal study is a critical component in helping you see how the beliefs you are studying are reflected in the pages of the Bible, so be sure to complete this study during the week before your next group meeting.**

Group Size

Think Like Jesus is designed to be experienced in a group setting such as a Bible study, Sunday school class, or any small-group gathering. To ensure everyone has enough time to participate in discussions, it is recommended that large groups watch the video together and then break up into smaller groups of four to six people for discussion.

Materials Needed

Each participant should have his or her own study guide. Although the course can be fully experienced with just the video and study guide, participants are also encouraged to have a copy of *Believe: Living the Story of the Bible to Become Like Jesus*, which includes selections from the *New International Version* that relate to each week's session. Reading *Believe* as you go through the study will provide even deeper insights and make the journey even richer and more meaningful.

Facilitation

Each group should appoint a leader who is responsible for starting the video and for keeping track of time during discussions and activities. Leaders may also read questions aloud and monitor discussions, prompting participants to respond and ensuring that everyone has the opportunity to participate. (For more thorough instructions, see the Leader's Guide included at the back of this guide.)

Session 1

WHO IS GOD?

A little girl in kindergarten was drawing a picture when her teacher walked up to her desk to take a look. She asked the child, "What are you drawing?" The bright-eyed girl quickly responded, "God." The teacher smiled and then said, "Well, honey, no one actually knows what God looks like." The child looked up from her work and confidently quipped, "Well then, they're about to!" This little girl had no doubts at all as to whether God exists—rather, she was now going to show the world what he looked like to her. This is exactly where we must begin in examining our belief in God—not with, "Does he exist?" but with, "Who is he?"

— VIDEO TEACHING NOTES —

Welcome to session one of *Think Like Jesus*. If this is your first time together as a group, take a moment to introduce yourselves to each other. As you watch the video, use the following outline to record some of the main points. (The answer key is found at the end of the session.)

- A. W. Tozer wrote, "What comes into our minds when we think about God is the most important thing about us." Why? Because this mindset—or absence of it—will drive all we _____ and all we _____ .

- **Key Question**: Who is _____?

- "For since the creation of the world God's invisible qualities—his eternal power and divine nature—have been clearly seen, being understood from what has been made, so that people are _____ _____ " (Romans 1:20).

- **Key Idea**: I believe the God of the Bible is the one _____ —Father, Son, and Holy Spirit.

- God is three persons who _____ a being.

- **Key Verse**: "May the grace of the Lord _____ _____ , and the love of _____, and the fellowship of the _____ _____ be with you all" (2 Corinthians 13:14).

- **(Key Application #1)**: Because God is God . . . I am
  _____ ; He is in _____ and in control; I
  want to know and follow his _____ for my life.

- **(Key Application #2)**: Because I was created in the
  image of God and for community . . . I recognize
  others' full _____ and respect boundaries;
  I look out for the rights, preferences, and _____
  of others; I _____ and enjoy others.

GETTING STARTED

Begin your discussion by reciting the key verse and key idea
together as a group. On your first attempt, use your notes if
you need help. On your second attempt, try to state them
completely from memory.

KEY VERSE: "May the grace of the Lord Jesus Christ,
and the love of God, and the fellowship of the Holy
Spirit be with you all" (2 Corinthians 13:14).

KEY IDEA: I believe the God of the Bible is the one
true God—Father, Son, and Holy Spirit.

GROUP DISCUSSION

As a group, discuss your thoughts and feelings about the following declarations. Which statements are easy to declare with certainty? Which are more challenging? Why?

- I believe the God of the Bible is the one true God.
- I believe the God of the Bible is one in essence but distinct in person—Father, Son and Holy Spirit.
- I believe Jesus is God in flesh—who died and rose bodily from the dead.
- I believe the Holy Spirit is God and dwells in Christians to empower them to live the Christian life.

Based on your group's dynamics and spiritual maturity, choose the two to three questions that will lead to the best discussion about this week's key idea.

1. If you only had two minutes to answer the question, "Who is God?" how would you respond?

2. How does your understanding of God impact your day-to-day decisions?

3. What are the most common reasons people struggle to believe that the God of the Bible is the one true God? What helped you get past these obstacles? Or, what obstacles are you still facing?

_____

_____

_____

_____

Read Luke 3:1–22 and choose one to two questions that will lead to the greatest discussion in your group.

1. In what ways is the Trinity a challenging concept for people to comprehend?

_____

_____

_____

_____

2. If God (the Trinity) is a community within himself, and if you are made in his image, then what does that tell you about yourself?

_____

_____

_____

_____

3. How does today's culture help or hinder you from experiencing the community for which you were created?

_____

_____

_____

_____

4. What specific actions can this group undertake to create healthy community?

_____

_____

_____

_____

CASE STUDY

Use the following case study as a model for a real-life situation where you might put this week's key idea into practice.

Mike is one of your favorite coworkers. He is funny, hardworking, and passionate about life. As a new Christian, he comes to you seeking help, because he and his wife are struggling. They are constantly butting heads, arguing, and simply not getting along. Mike thinks it is just easier to walk away but really wants to know what you think.

Using the following key applications from this session, what gentle advice would you give Mike?

KEY APPLICATION #1: Because God is God, I am not. He is in charge and in control. I want to know and follow his will for my life.

KEY APPLICATION #2: Because I was created in the image of God and for community, I recognize others' full personhood and respect boundaries. I look out for the rights, preferences, and comforts of others. I value and enjoy others.

CLOSING PRAYER

Close your time together with prayer. Share your prayer requests with one another. Ask God to help you put this week's key idea into practice.

FOR NEXT WEEK

Before your next group meeting, be sure to read through the following personal study and complete the exercises.

VIDEO NOTES ANSWER KEY

are, do / God / without excuse / true God / share / Jesus Christ, God, Holy Spirit / not, charge, will / personhood, comforts, value

PERSONAL STUDY

Every session in this guide contains a personal study to help you make meaningful connections between your life and what you are learning each week. Take some time after your group meeting each week to read through this section and complete the personal study. In total, the personal study should take about one hour to complete. Some people like to spread it out, devoting about ten to fifteen minutes a day. Others choose one larger block of time during the week to work through the entire personal study in one sitting. There is no right or wrong way to do this! Just choose a plan that best fits your needs and schedule from week to week, and then allow the Scripture to take root in your heart.

KEY QUESTION
WHO IS GOD?

Any discussion regarding this big idea will have to start with the question, "Who is God?" The Bible's first words are, "In the beginning God . . ." (Genesis 1:1). Our very lives, as a part of this story, also begin with God as our Creator.

The story of the world's beginning has no hint of defense. No language flirting with a desire to prove. No attempt to allow for anything other than this overarching truth being true. The entire Bible from Genesis to Revelation is written on the assumption there is a God—the constant focal character of each story.

The apostle Paul writes, "For since the creation of the world God's invisible qualities—his eternal power and divine nature—have been clearly seen, being understood from what has been made, so that people are without excuse" (Romans 1:20). So, our central question here is not, "Is there a God?" but, "Who is the one true God?"

In the beginning God created the heavens and the earth (Genesis 1:1).

The heavens declare the glory of God; the skies proclaim the work of his hands. Day after day they pour forth speech; night after night they reveal knowledge. They have no speech, they use no words; no sound is heard from them. Yet their voice goes out into all the earth, their words to the ends of the world. In the heavens God has pitched a tent for the sun (Psalm 19:1–4).

For since the creation of the world God's invisible qualities— his eternal power and divine nature—have been clearly seen, being understood from what has been made, so that people are without excuse (Romans 1:20).

1. What is significant about the way the Bible begins?

_____

_____

_____

_____

_____

2. How has God revealed his invisible qualities since the creation of the world?

_____

_____

_____

_____

KEY IDEA
ONE TRUE GOD IN THREE PERSONS

Throughout the Old Testament, the clarion call is for belief in the oneness of God. The *Shema* (Hebrew for "hear") forms the belief without mincing words: "Hear, O Israel: The LORD our God, the LORD is one" (Deuteronomy 6:4). Yet, as we turn the page to the New Testament, the names of what seem to be three deities emerge—God the Father, God the Son, and God the Holy Spirit. These three are mentioned and appear throughout the Old Testament era, but their distinctive identity and presence invade the life and times of the New Testament.

To reconcile this mathematical equation of 3 = 1, theologians invented the word *Trinity* (a word not used in the Bible) to capture God's essence—three persons who share a being, or fundamental nature. Throughout the centuries, students of the Bible have come up with analogies to get at the heart of the nature of God as a Trinity and to make it a more accessible and practical concept. The following has helped me in developing a practical concept for the nature of God and in understanding what it means to be made in God's image.

The one true God—Father, Son, and Holy Spirit—created humans in their image as a community (see Genesis 1:26-27).

And we are told the two have become one (see Genesis 2:24). Our true nature is like God. We were not only created *for* community but we *are* a community. When we enter a relationship with God through Christ, we are placed in the body of Christ (see 1 Corinthians 12:27). We, though we are many, become one (see Romans 12:4–5). In this way, Christ restores our reflection of the nature of God that was lost in the Garden of Eden. Now you can understand why relationships are so important to God!

Now the LORD God had formed out of the ground all the wild animals and all the birds in the sky. He brought them to the man to see what he would name them; and whatever the man called each living creature, that was its name. So the man gave names to all the livestock, the birds in the sky and all the wild animals.

But for Adam no suitable helper was found. So the LORD God caused the man to fall into a deep sleep; and while he was sleeping, he took one of the man's ribs and then closed up the place with flesh. Then the LORD God made a woman from the rib he had taken out of the man, and he brought her to the man.

The man said, "This is now bone of my bones and flesh of my flesh; she shall be called 'woman,' for she was taken out of man." That is why a man leaves his father and mother and is united to his wife, and they become one flesh (Genesis 2:19–24).

In the beginning was the Word, and the Word was with God, and the Word was God. He was with God in the beginning. Through him all things were made; without him nothing was made that has been made. In him was life, and that life was the light of all mankind. The light shines in the darkness, and the darkness has not overcome it (John 1:1–5).

When all the people were being baptized, Jesus was baptized too. And as he was praying, heaven was opened and the Holy Spirit descended on him in bodily form like a dove. And a voice came from heaven: "You are my Son, whom I love; with you I am well pleased" (Luke 3:21–22).

1. How do you personally wrap your mind around the idea of the Trinity?

2. In what ways have you experienced God as Father? As Jesus the Son? As the Holy Spirit?

KEY APPLICATION
WHAT DIFFERENCE THIS MAKES

If we embrace the God of the Bible as the one true God, we will realize that we are *not* God and that he is in charge and in control. We will want to know and follow his will for our lives.

Likewise, if we embrace the "three-ness" of God as Father, Son, and Holy Spirit, we will observe how they treat each other and seek to emulate these principles in our relationships with each other. We will recognize the full personhood of others and respect boundaries, look out for their rights and preferences, and learn to value and enjoy them.

For any situation, relationship, or decision that we face, we can resolutely apply these principles to guide us. The results, over time, will lead to blessing in our own souls in the form of fruit such as joy and peace, and we will express our actions outwardly for others to enjoy in the form of fruit such as love and kindness.

Paul then stood up in the meeting of the Areopagus and said: "People of Athens! I see that in every way you are very religious. For as I walked around and looked carefully at your objects of worship, I even found an altar with this inscription: TO AN UNKNOWN GOD. *So you are ignorant of the very thing you worship—and this is what I am going to proclaim to you.*

"The God who made the world and everything in it is the Lord of heaven and earth and does not live in temples built by human hands. And he is not served by human hands, as if he needed anything. Rather, he himself gives everyone life and breath and everything else. From one man he made all the nations, that they should inhabit the whole earth; and he marked out their appointed times in history and the boundaries of their lands. God did this so that they would seek him and perhaps reach out for him and find him, though he is not far from any one of us. 'For in him we live and move and have our being.' As some of your own poets have said, 'We are his offspring.'

"Therefore since we are God's offspring, we should not think that the divine being is like gold or silver or stone—an image made by human design and skill. In the past God overlooked such ignorance, but now he commands all people everywhere to repent. For he has set a day when he will judge the world with justice by the man he has appointed. He has given proof of this to everyone by raising him from the dead" (Acts 17:22–31).

1. What is meant by the phrase Paul quoted: "For in him we live and move and have our being"?

2. How does your understanding of who God is affect your character?

EVALUATE

As you conclude this personal study, use a scale of 1–6 to rate how strongly you believe the following statements (1 = no belief at all, 6 = complete confidence):

_____ I believe the God of the Bible is the only true God.

_____ I believe the God of the Bible is one in essence but distinct in person—Father, Son, and Holy Spirit.

_____ I believe Jesus is God in the flesh—who died and rose bodily from the dead.

_____ I believe the Holy Spirit is God and dwells in Christians to empower them to live the Christian life.

TAKE ACTION

Memorizing Scripture is a valuable discipline for all believers to exercise. Spend a few minutes each day committing this week's key verse to memory.

KEY VERSE: "May the grace of the Lord Jesus Christ, and the love of God, and the fellowship of the Holy Spirit be with you all" (2 Corinthians 13:14).

Recite this week's key idea out loud. As you do, ask yourself, _Does my life reflect this statement?_

KEY IDEA: I believe the God of the Bible is the one true God—Father, Son, and Holy Spirit.

Answer the following questions to help you apply this week's key idea to your own life.

1. What behaviors help you recognize someone who believes the God of the Bible is the one true God?

2. What, if anything, hinders you from putting your faith solely in the God of the Bible?

3. What is something you can do this week to demonstrate your belief in the one true God?

Session 2

DOES GOD CARE ABOUT ME?

Once we declare the God of the Bible to be the only true God—Father, Son, and Holy Spirit—the next question becomes, "Is he good?" Or, to state the question another way, "Does God care about us personally?" In the Bible, we find that the answer is a definitive *yes.* God reveals his care by displaying his goodness to the world, by revealing his plan for our lives, and by displaying his care for his creation. The Bible is our source for seeing God at work throughout the ages, and it reveals that because of God's love and care in the past, we can rely on the goodness of his character to be unchanging for us in the present and into the future.

VIDEO TEACHING NOTES

Welcome to session two of *Think Like Jesus*. If there are any new members in your group, take a moment to introduce yourselves to each other. Spend a few minutes sharing any insights or questions about last week's personal study. Then start the video and use the following outline to record some of the main points. (The answer key is found at the end of the session.)

- **Key Question:** Does God _____ about me?

- **Key Idea:** I believe God is _____ in and _____ about my daily life.

- "The LORD is my shepherd, I lack nothing. He _____ me lie down in green pastures, he _____ me beside quiet waters, he _____ my soul. He _____ me along the right paths for his name's sake. Even though I walk through the darkest valley, I will fear no evil, for you are _____ me; your rod and your staff, they _____ me. You _____ a table before me in the presence of my enemies. You _____ my head with oil; my cup overflows. Surely your goodness and love will follow me all the days of my life, and I will dwell in the house of the LORD forever" (Psalm 23:1–6).

- **Key Verse:** "I lift up my eyes to the mountains— where does my _____ come from? My _____ comes from the LORD, the Maker of heaven and earth" (Psalm 121:1-2).

- (Key Application #1): Be _____ : God's ways are higher than my ways.

- (Key Application #2): Don't _____ : God, who controls nature and history, cares about me.

- (Key Application #3): Be _____ : God is working out his good plan for my life.

GETTING STARTED

Begin your discussion by reciting the key verse and key idea together as a group. On your first attempt, use your notes if you need help. On your second attempt, try to state them completely from memory.

KEY VERSE: "I lift up my eyes to the mountain— where does my help come from? My help comes from the LORD, the Maker of heaven and earth" (Psalm 121:1-2).

KEY IDEA: I believe God is involved in and cares about my daily life.

GROUP DISCUSSION

As a group, discuss your thoughts and feelings about the following declarations. Which statements are easy to declare with certainty? Which are more challenging? Why?

- I believe God has a purpose for my life.
- I believe pain and suffering can often bring me closer to God.
- I believe God is actively involved in my life.
- I believe God enables me to do things I could not or would not otherwise do.

Based on your group's dynamics and spiritual maturity, choose the two to three questions that will lead to the best discussion about this week's key idea.

1. Have you ever asked yourself, "Does God care about me?" If so, what experience or thought helped formulate your answer?

2. What are some specific ways that you experience God in your daily life?

3. What activities or disciplines heighten your awareness of God's activity in your life?

Read Psalm 23:1–6 and choose one to two questions that will lead to the greatest discussion in your group.

1. This psalm describes God as a good shepherd who leads, guides, refreshes, comforts, prepares, and anoints us. Which action best describes your interactions with God?

2. How does freedom from worry demonstrate your confidence in God's ability to provide and care for you?

3. Why is it challenging to trust that God's ways are higher than your ways? How can you overcome these obstacles?

4. What thoughts and emotions come to mind when you consider that God has a good plan for your life?

_____

_____

_____

_____

CASE STUDY

Use the following case study as a model for a real-life situation where you might put this week's key idea into practice.

> Jill has been part of a church community for as long as she can remember. But secretly, she has struggled with doubts about God's will for her life. In a moment of vulnerability, she confesses to you that she fears she will never get married or have a family of her own. Her questions can be summed up this way: (1) How can I be certain that God's will for me is good? (2) Why would the God of the universe care about the details of my life?

Using the following key applications from this session, what could you do to help Jill find the answers to her questions?

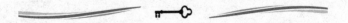

KEY APPLICATION #1: Be mindful: God's ways are higher than my ways.

KEY APPLICATION #2: Don't worry: God, who controls nature and history, cares about me.

KEY APPLICATION #3: Be excited: God is working out his good plan for my life.

CLOSING PRAYER

Close your time together with prayer. Share your prayer requests with one another. Ask God to help you put this week's key idea into practice.

FOR NEXT WEEK

Before your next group meeting, be sure to read through the following personal study and complete the exercises.

VIDEO NOTES ANSWER KEY

care / makes, leads, refreshes, guides, with, comfort, prepare, anoint / help, help / involved, cares / mindful / worry / excited

PERSONAL STUDY

Last week you took a look at your beliefs about who God is—Father, Son, and Holy Spirit. Perhaps you learned something about God or about yourself that you never knew before. Before your next group meeting, complete the following study. Allow the Scripture to take root in your heart and then evaluate your feelings about how God is involved in your daily life.

KEY QUESTION
IS GOD GOOD?

After witnessing a human tragedy, some people conclude, "I don't believe there is a God. No God would allow bad things to happen to good people." This line of reason states that if negative events occur, or if things seem out of control, it must mean there is no God in charge. The reality, of course, is that God doesn't have to be good to exist. However, according the Bible, not only is he good but he also desires to have a personal relationship with us.

Another line of reasoning states that the suffering and trials we experience in this life indicate that God is uninvolved with his creation. Adherents to this way of thinking suggest that bad things happen because God created the universe to be like some form of cosmic watch. He just wound it up and then let the earth and the universe run on the natural laws he set in place.

However, when we read the Bible from beginning to end, we find that God is involved in and cares about every aspect of our daily lives. In addition, as we will see in a later session, he makes it clear that his followers will experience future eternity with him when this life is over—a place where there will be "no more death or mourning or crying or pain" (Revelation 21:4).

Even in this life, God will take our trials and our tragedies and turn them into something good (see Genesis 50:20). He does this because he is a compassionate and personal God.

> I lift up my eyes to the mountains—
>   where does my help come from?
> My help comes from the LORD,
>   the Maker of heaven and earth (Psalm 121:1-2).

> She gave this name to the LORD who spoke to her: "You are the God who sees me," for she said, "I have now seen the One who sees me" (Genesis 16:13).

> When I consider your heavens,
>   the work of your fingers,
> the moon and the stars,
>   which you have set in place,
> what is mankind that you are mindful of them,
>   human beings that you care for them?
> (Psalm 8:3-4).

1. What opinions have you heard expressed about whether God is good?

_____

_____

_____

_____

2. Why is it important to know that God is good?

_____

_____

_____

_____

KEY IDEA
I BELIEVE GOD IS INVOLVED IN AND CARES ABOUT MY DAILY LIFE

The Bible reveals several key concepts about the qualities of God. First, God is above us, or "transcendent." He is not bound by any of the circumstances or events that happen in this world. He has created everything, so he therefore has complete authority over everything. He is in complete control of our universe, and nothing that happens is a surprise to him.

Given this, we might wonder why a God who has everything cares about us personally. The answer to this question leads us to the second quality about God: he chooses to be near to us, or "immanent." Although God is above the fray and cares of this life, he desires to draw near to us. He comes down and stoops to our level to meet us where we are. Our great God is able to draw close to us, to care for us, and to love us at a depth we struggle to grasp.

But there's more. The third quality of God states that he has a plan for us, or is "provident." God doesn't just intervene at times and places to get us out of a jam. He has a predetermined plan for our lives that is set in motion at the moment of our creation. And that plan God is working out for those who trust him and follow him is *good*.

> *I praise you because I am fearfully and wonderfully made;*
> > *your works are wonderful,*
> > *I know that full well.*
> *My frame was not hidden from you*
> > *when I was made in the secret place,*
> > *when I was woven together in the depths of the earth.*
> *Your eyes saw my unformed body;*
> > *all the days ordained for me were written in your book*
> > *before one of them came to be.*
> *How precious to me are your thoughts, God!*
> > *How vast is the sum of them!*
> *Were I to count them,*
> > *they would outnumber the grains of sand—*
> > *when I awake, I am still with you*
> (Psalm 139:14–18).

> *Being confident of this, that he who began a good work in you will carry it on to completion until the day of Christ Jesus* (Philippians 1:6).

And we know that in all things God works for the good of those who love him, who have been called according to his purpose (Romans 8:28).

1. Why is it important to recognize all three qualities of God—that he is above you, that he is near you, and that he has a plan for you?

_____

_____

_____

_____

2. How does God's care for you help you to know him better?

_____

_____

_____

_____

KEY APPLICATION
WHAT DIFFERENCE THIS MAKES

Our confidence that God's ways are higher than our ways, and that he controls nature and history, allows us to rest in his care. God uses the distance between heaven and earth to teach us the breadth and depth of his being. We are often tempted to make decisions because we can't see what is in the road ahead. But when we feel this way, we must remember that God has a different vantage point from his throne . . . and we must trust in his plans and timing.

Jesus conveyed God's care for us throughout the Gospels and encouraged us to live free from worry (see Matthew 6:25–34). He shows us that God is not out to get us but to redeem us—not to destroy us but to restore us. This is the heart of a loving Father. As we come to realize this, we can know every morning as we wake up that his heart is to show us his plan and include us in his big picture. We can know that in the tough times, he will see us through and draw us ever closer to him. He will hear our prayers and see our tears.

God's heart is to keep us close to him, no matter what circumstances we may be walking through. We can seek God and ask him for wisdom, knowing that every good gift that we receive comes from his hands. When we grasp these foundational beliefs in our minds and hearts, we are able to walk through each day with joy, hope, and confidence.

> *"For my thoughts are not your thoughts,*
> *neither are your ways my ways,"*
> *declares the* LORD.
> *"As the heavens are higher than the earth,*
> *so are my ways higher than your ways*
> *and my thoughts than your thoughts"*
> (Isaiah 55:8–9).

> *"So do not worry, saying, 'What shall we eat?' or 'What shall we drink?' or 'What shall we wear?' For the pagans run after all these things, and your heavenly Father knows that you need them. But seek first his kingdom and his righteousness, and all these things will be given to you as well.*

Therefore do not worry about tomorrow, for tomorrow will worry about itself. Each day has enough trouble of its own" (Matthew 6:31–34).

Humble yourselves, therefore, under God's mighty hand, that he may lift you up in due time. Cast all your anxiety on him because he cares for you (1 Peter 5:6–7).

Don't be deceived, my dear brothers and sisters. Every good and perfect gift is from above, coming down from the Father of the heavenly lights, who does not change like shifting shadows (James 1:16–17).

1. How does freedom from worry demonstrate your confidence in God's care?

   _____

   _____

   _____

   _____

   _____

2. What does it mean to trust in God's goodness and care for you?

   _____

   _____

   _____

   _____

   _____

   _____

EVALUATE

As you conclude this personal study, use a scale of 1–6 to rate how strongly you believe the following statements (1 = no belief at all, 6 = complete confidence):

_____ I believe God has a purpose for my life.
_____ I believe pain and suffering can often bring me closer to God.
_____ I believe God is actively involved in my life.
_____ I believe God enables me to do things I could not or would not otherwise do.

TAKE ACTION

Memorizing Scripture is a valuable discipline for all believers to exercise. Spend a few minutes each day committing this week's key verse to memory.

KEY VERSE: "I lift up my eyes to the mountain— where does my help come from? My help comes from the LORD, the Maker of heaven and earth" (Psalm 121:1–2).

Recite this week's key idea out loud. As you do, ask yourself, *Does my life reflect this statement?*

KEY IDEA: I believe God is involved in and cares about my daily life.

Answer the following questions to help you apply this week's key idea to your own life.

1. How would this belief express itself in your life?

   _____

   _____

   _____

   _____

   _____

2. What visible attributes can be found in someone who is personally connected to God?

   _____

   _____

   _____

3. What is impeding your ability to experience God in a personal way? How can you overcome these obstacles?

   _____

   _____

   _____

4. What action step can you take this week to increase your awareness of God's involvement in your daily life?

   _____

   _____

   _____

   _____

Session 3

HOW DO I HAVE A RELATIONSHIP WITH GOD?

What does it mean to be *saved*? Is a simple prayer really sufficient to give us a relationship with God and entrance into heaven? What salvation through Jesus means is the most important query in all of life. It is literally a matter of life and death. For this reason, we need to take a close look at the Bible—without the trappings of tradition and preconceived ideas—to see what God has to say about this important subject. In particular, we need to examine what God says about the problem of sin, so we can see the solution he has provided to overcome the problem. The beautiful outcome of solving this problem transforms our lives today and for eternity!

VIDEO TEACHING NOTES

Welcome to session three of *Think Like Jesus*. Spend a few minutes sharing any insights or questions about last week's personal study. Then start the video and use the following outline to record some of the main points. (The answer key is found at the end of the session.)

- **Key Question:** How do I have a _____ with God?

- _____ is found in Jesus.

- **Key Idea:** I believe a person comes into a _____ _____ relationship with God by God's _____ through _____ in Jesus Christ.

- **Key Verse:** "For it is by _____ you have been saved, through _____ — and this is not from yourselves, it is the gift of God—not by works, so that no one can boast" (Ephesians 2:8–9).

- In order for the sacrifice of Christ to be applied to us individually, we must reach out and _____ _____ it by faith.

- (Key Application #1): No matter what _____ I face in this life, they pale in comparison to my salvation for eternity.

- (Key Application #2): I need to walk in _____ and _____ grace to others.

GETTING STARTED

Begin your discussion by reciting the key verse and key idea together as a group. On your first attempt, use your notes if you need help. On your second attempt, try to state them completely from memory.

KEY VERSE: "For it is by grace you have been saved, through faith—and this is not from yourselves, it is the gift of God—not by works, so that no one can boast" (Ephesians 2:8–9).

KEY IDEA: I believe a person comes into a right relationship with God by God's grace through faith in Jesus Christ.

GROUP DISCUSSION

As a group, discuss your thoughts and feelings about the following declarations. Which statements are easy to declare with certainty? Which are more challenging? Why?

- I believe I will inherit eternal life because of what Jesus has done for me.
- I believe nothing I do or have done can earn my salvation.
- I believe salvation comes only through Jesus.
- I believe people are saved because of what Jesus did, not because of what they do.

Based on your group's dynamics and spiritual maturity, choose the two to three questions that will lead to the best discussion about this week's key idea.

1. How would you define the word *grace*? What is the opposite of grace?

2. What would it look like for you to offer grace to people who don't deserve it, as God did for you?

3. Without naming names, who is someone who doesn't deserve your love and kindness, but you offer it anyway?

4. Many people today find it hard to receive something they didn't earn. How could this attitude hinder a person's spiritual growth?

_____

_____

_____

_____

_____

Read Genesis 3:1–24 and Romans 5:12–21 and choose one to two questions that will lead to the greatest discussion in your group.

1. How did Adam and Eve's decision to disobey God affect all of humankind?

_____

_____

_____

_____

_____

2. How did Jesus' choices overturn the effect of Adam and Eve's sin in our lives?

_____

_____

_____

_____

_____

3. What do these passages tell you about the character of God and his feelings toward you and all of humanity?

_____

_____

_____

CASE STUDY

Use the following case study as a model for a real-life situation where you might put this week's key idea into practice.

> Rocky is a real man's man. There is nothing he can't fix. He spends more time tinkering in his garage than in his own house. Luckily, he's your neighbor, so when you break something, he is always willing to lend a hand. One day in a moment of authenticity, he confesses that he has never quite understood God and religion but knows he needs them. Yet he fears that his past mistakes have disqualified him from ever being what he calls a "religious person."

Using the following key applications from this session, discuss how you can reveal the misconceptions that Rocky has about God's character and point him to the truth.

KEY APPLICATION #1: No matter what troubles I face in this life, they pale in comparison to my salvation for eternity.

KEY APPLICATION #2: I need to walk in grace and offer grace to others.

CLOSING PRAYER

Close your time together with prayer. Share your prayer requests with one another. Ask God to help you put this week's key idea into practice.

FOR NEXT WEEK

Before your next group meeting, be sure to read through the following personal study and complete the exercises.

VIDEO NOTES ANSWER KEY

relationship / salvation / right, grace, faith / grace, faith / receive / troubles / grace, offer

PERSONAL STUDY

Last week you took a look at your beliefs about how God is involved in your daily life. Perhaps you were able to reflect on how God really does care about your daily activities. Before your next group meeting, complete the following study. Allow the Scripture to take root in your heart as you consider what salvation through Jesus means to you.

KEY QUESTION
HOW DO I HAVE A RELATIONSHIP WITH GOD?

A rich man once asked Jesus, "What must I do to inherit eternal life?" (Mark 10:17). Jesus replied that he needed to keep God's commandments. The man responded by saying he had been keeping the law since he was a boy. But then Jesus said, "One thing you lack . . . go, sell everything you have and give to the poor" (verse 21).

At first glance, Jesus' words seem to indicate that if we want to have a relationship with God, we need to *do good works* for him. However, in truth Jesus is not emphasizing salvation by works but a scriptural progression of thought. Jesus was showing the man that he had never—and could never—keep the law perfectly and inherit eternal life. Jesus was giving the man an opportunity to express faith and receive grace by following him.

Often, we try to be good enough, through our works, to deserve a relationship with God. But that never works. The only one who was ever good enough to perfectly follow the law was Jesus. So, he chose to fulfill all the requirements of the law perfectly on our behalf. All we have to do is believe with our hearts, and profess out loud with our mouths, that he is our Lord (see Romans 10:9–10). God makes us this offer solely on the basis of his grace. Our good works then become a manifestation of the relationship we have with God.

Salvation is from Christ alone, and our acceptance of his gift must genuinely come from the expression of faith from the heart.

For it is by grace you have been saved, through faith—and this is not from yourselves, it is the gift of God—not by works, so that no one can boast (Ephesians 2:8–9).

"Very truly I tell you, no one can enter the kingdom of God unless they are born of water and the Spirit." . . . *For God so loved the world that he gave his one and only Son, that whoever believes in him shall not perish but have eternal life. For God did not send his Son into the world to condemn the world, but to save the world through him* (John 3:5, 16–17).

If you declare with your mouth, "Jesus is Lord," and believe in your heart that God raised him from the dead, you will be saved. For it is with your heart that you believe and are justified, and it is with your mouth that you profess your faith and are saved (Romans 10:9–10).

1. What is required for you to have a relationship with God and receive eternal life?

_____

_____

_____

_____

2. Why is it important to both believe in our hearts and profess with our mouths that Jesus is Lord?

_____

_____

_____

_____

KEY IDEA

I BELIEVE A PERSON COMES INTO A RIGHT RELATIONSHIP WITH GOD BY GOD'S GRACE THROUGH FAITH IN JESUS CHRIST

While there are many points of doctrine in the Bible that may be difficult to understand, salvation is not one of them. We all need salvation because we all sin (see Romans 3:23). Sin causes death—both the physical death of our bodies and the spiritual death of our separation from God (see Romans 6:23). God made his solution to this problem abundantly clear and profoundly simple: "Salvation is found in no one else, for there is no other name under heaven given to mankind by which we must be saved" (Acts 4:12).

Over the centuries, Christians have been unified that salvation is not something we can earn or that we deserve. God extends salvation through his *grace*—which means receiving something we don't deserve. Jesus also made it clear that it is only through him that we can receive salvation (see John 14:6). The fact that God provides a way to know him is an illustration of his love for us. Without this opportunity, we would be hopeless and lost.

The Bible is also clear that salvation is not unconditional reconciliation for all humans. There will be a time of final judgment. Sadly, not everyone chooses to accept the gift of salvation that God offers so they can gain access into his eternal kingdom. Yet the offer of salvation remains available to all, regardless of their past, for as long as they are on this earth.

> But he was pierced for our transgressions,
>   he was crushed for our iniquities;
> the punishment that brought us peace was on him,
>   and by his wounds we are healed (Isaiah 53:5).

> For the wages of sin is death, but the gift of God is eternal life in Christ Jesus our Lord (Romans 6:23).

> "No! We believe it is through the grace of our Lord Jesus that we are saved, just as they are" (Acts 15:11).

> Jesus answered, "I am the way and the truth and the life. No one comes to the Father except through me" (John 14:6).

1. Why do people need salvation through Jesus Christ?

_____

_____

_____

_____

2. How is God's grace a key element in the salvation God offers us?

_____

_____

_____

_____

KEY APPLICATION
WHAT DIFFERENCE THIS MAKES

No matter what troubles we face in this life, they pale in comparison to our salvation for eternity. This is an attitude faithful Christians have lived out throughout the ages. Persecution for their faith, poor health, or the pain of broken relationships could not compare to the future glory they knew awaited them. Adopting this same mindset allows the Holy Spirit to strengthen us as we face troubles and influence how God can use our circumstances. Our thankful hearts, in spite of our current situation, show that we value God's sacrifice of his Son, Jesus.

Now, as we enjoy what God has done in our lives, it would be wrong for us to refuse to offer forgiveness and grace to someone else. Furthermore, it would be wrong for us to not share the love of God that is within us to others. As we look at others through God's eyes of compassion and love, we should be compelled to share our story of faith. Extending grace to others may not only save their lives, but it will also please God and build his church. We have been given the greatest gift we could ever hope to receive: eternal life through salvation in Christ. We need to share that news with a world that desperately needs to hear it.

> *I have been crucified with Christ and I no longer live, but Christ lives in me. The life I now live in the body, I live by faith in the Son of God, who loved me and gave himself for me. I do not set aside the grace of God, for if righteousness could be gained through the law, Christ died for nothing!"* (Galatians 2:20–21).

> *Since we have that same spirit of faith, we also believe and therefore speak, because we know that the one who raised the Lord Jesus from the dead will also raise us with Jesus and present us with you to himself. All this is for your benefit, so that the grace that is reaching more and more people may cause thanksgiving to overflow to the glory of God* (2 Corinthians 4:13–15).

1. What is your reaction when you consider that Jesus died for your sins and has offered you eternal life?

   _____

   _____

   _____

2. What opportunities has God provided to you personally to extend his grace to others?

   _____

   _____

   _____

EVALUATE

As you conclude this personal study, use a scale of 1–6 to rate how strongly you believe the following statements (1 = no belief at all, 6 = complete confidence):

_____ I believe I will inherit eternal life because of what Jesus has done for me.

_____ I believe nothing I do or have done can earn my salvation.

_____ I believe salvation comes only through Jesus.

_____ I believe people are saved because of what Jesus did, not because of what they do.

TAKE ACTION

Memorizing Scripture is a valuable discipline for all believers to exercise. Spend a few minutes each day committing this week's key verse to memory.

KEY VERSE: "For it is by grace you have been saved, through faith—and this is not from yourselves, it is the gift of God—not by works, so that no one can boast" (Ephesians 2:8–9).

Recite this week's key idea out loud. As you do, ask yourself, _Does my life reflect this statement?_

KEY IDEA: I believe a person comes into a right relationship with God by God's grace through faith in Jesus Christ.

Answer the following questions to help you apply this week's key idea to your own life.

1. How would this belief express itself in your life?

2. What visible attributes can be found in someone who has received the gift of salvation?

3. If you haven't confessed with your mouth that Jesus is Lord and believed in your heart that he has risen from the dead, what is keeping you from doing so?

4. Is there someone in your life who needs to know about salvation by grace through faith in Jesus? What, if anything, is stopping you from having that conversation?

_____

_____

_____

_____

_____

_____

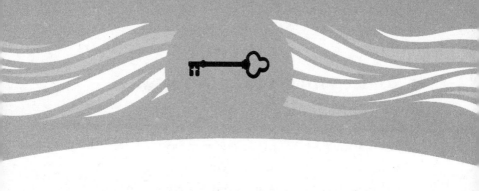

Session 4

HOW DOES THE BIBLE GUIDE MY LIFE?

WELCOME

A story is told of the night the Green Bay Packers lost an away game they were expected to win. After the team took the long bus ride back home, legendary coach Vince Lombardi had the players put their sweaty uniforms back on and march out onto Lambeau Field. He huddled them together, held up an egg-shaped object high in the air, and said, "Gentlemen, this is a football!" Vince Lombardi knew one of the fundamentals of winning a football game is having a firm grasp of the basics. The same is true of the Christian life. So, in the spirit of an unforgettable night in bitterly cold Wisconsin, I hold up a black leather book and say to you, "Ladies and gentlemen, this is a Bible!" But why is this book so important and essential?

VIDEO TEACHING NOTES

Welcome to session four of *Think Like Jesus*. Spend a few minutes sharing any insights or questions about last week's personal study. Then start the video and use the following outline to record some of the main points. (The answer key is found at the end of the session.)

- **Key Question**: How do I know God and his _____ for my life?

- **Key Idea**: I believe the Bible is the _____ _____ and has the right to command my belief and action.

- **Key Verse**: "All Scripture is God-breathed and is useful for _____ , _____ , _____ and _____ in righteousness, so that the servant of God may be thoroughly equipped for every good work" (2 Timothy 3:16–17).

- The psalmist writes: "Your word is a _____ for my feet, a _____ on my path" (Psalm 119:105).

- (**Key Application #1**): The Bible is the _____ from which I view the world.

- (**Key Application #2**): I am motivated to study the Bible to _____ God's will for my life.

- (**Key Application #3**): The principles in the Bible must _____ my life even when I don't fully understand or like what it teaches.

GETTING STARTED

Begin your discussion by reciting the key verse and key idea together as a group. On your first attempt, use your notes if you need help. On your second attempt, try to state them completely from memory.

KEY VERSE: "All Scripture is God-breathed and is useful for teaching, rebuking, correcting and training in righteousness, so that the servant of God may be thoroughly equipped for every good work" (2 Timothy 3:16–17).

KEY IDEA: I believe the Bible is the Word of God and has the right to command my belief and action.

GROUP DISCUSSION

As a group, discuss your thoughts and feelings about the following declarations. Which statements are easy to declare with certainty? Which are more challenging? Why?

- I believe the Bible is absolutely true in matters of faith and morals.
- I believe the words of the Bible are words from God.
- I believe the Bible has decisive authority over what I say and do.
- I believe the Bible is relevant to address the needs of contemporary culture.

Based on your group's dynamics and spiritual maturity, choose the two to three questions that will lead to the best discussion about this week's key idea.

1. In what ways can the Bible inform and govern your decision making in the areas of business, family life, friendships, and recreation?

2. In what ways have you seen the Bible be useful for teaching, rebuking, correcting, and training?

3. How has understanding the Bible changed the way you see the world?

Read Exodus 20:1–21 and choose one to two questions that will lead to the greatest discussion in your group.

1. How do the Ten Commandments reveal what is most important to God?

2. How would the world be different if all of humanity were guided by the Bible?

3. What are some ways the Bible has clarified misconceptions you had about God's character?

4. How has the Bible given you a better understanding of who you are and your purpose in this world?

_____

_____

_____

_____

_____

CASE STUDY

Use the following case study as a model for a real-life situation where you might put this week's key idea into practice.

Suzanne is a college student who attends your Bible study that meets at the local coffee shop on Thursday mornings. As the group discusses prayer requests, Suzanne expresses her need for wisdom in balancing her busy schedule. In the next seven days, she has to study for finals, write a research paper, and work four shifts in the university bookstore.

A few days later, you call to check on her. She still sounds stressed but appreciates the call. "Do you think you will be able to get everything done?" you ask. "Yes, I've already taken two tests that went well, but I have one more that is really important. If I don't do well, I will have to take the class over again next semester. So, I'm thinking about using one of my roommate's research papers from last year. I'll change up the words a little so it sounds like me, but it will allow me more time to study for my test. I know it's kind of dishonest, but I don't see any other way to get everything done."

Using the following key applications from this session, discuss what you could say or do to help Suzanne see the importance of doing the right thing.

KEY APPLICATION #1: The Bible is the lens from which I view the world.

KEY APPLICATION #2: I am motivated to study the Bible to understand God's will for my life.

KEY APPLICATION #3: The principles in the Bible must govern my life even when I don't fully understand or like what it teaches.

CLOSING PRAYER

Close your time together with prayer. Share your prayer requests with one another. Ask God to help you put this week's key idea into practice.

FOR NEXT WEEK

Before your next group meeting, be sure to read through the following personal study and complete the exercises.

VIDEO NOTES ANSWER KEY

will / Word of God / teaching, rebuking, correcting, training / lamp, light / lens / understand / govern

PERSONAL STUDY

Last week you examined your beliefs about salvation. Perhaps you've been a Christian for a while, and you're discovering new things about what you believe. Or maybe you're new to the faith or simply exploring what it means to be a Christian. If so, feel free to ask questions and connect with your group leader or pastor for help. Before your next group meeting, complete the following study. Ask God to help you recognize the tremendous value of his Word.

KEY QUESTION
HOW CAN I KNOW GOD AND HIS WILL FOR MY LIFE?

As we look at the wonders of nature and the world around us, we can conclude there is a God. But how do we learn about this God? How do we come into a full relationship with him? What are his plans and purposes for us? What are the principles he wants us to live by? The answer to all these questions is found in God's revelation to us: the Bible. The Bible answers our questions about God's truth, but it also invites us to believe and embrace so much more.

As believers in Christ, it is critical for us to know with confidence that the Bible is the inspired Word of God and contains God's truth and will for our lives. It is also critical for us to know how to understand its truths for ourselves. The Bible helps us know important matters such as the identity of the one true God and his love for us. It helps us to realize we have been born into sin and are separated from God. It also reveals that Jesus paid for our sins in order to restore us. The Bible outlines the best way to live a successful and productive life and gives us the truth about the future and God's ultimate plan for the redemption of all people.

The Bible holds great power for Christians. God speaks to us through it because he loves us and wants us to have access to knowing him. The Word of God carries great power and authority because of the authority of the One who speaks it. God breathed life into things—including the words of the Bible—and he uses his Word to show us his purposes.

> As the rain and the snow
>   come down from heaven,
> and do not return to it
>   without watering the earth
> and making it bud and flourish,
>   so that it yields seed for the sower and bread for the eater,
> so is my word that goes out from my mouth:
>   It will not return to me empty,
> but will accomplish what I desire
>   and achieve the purpose for which I sent it
> (Isaiah 55:10–11).

> And beginning with Moses and all the Prophets, [Jesus] explained to them what was said in all the Scriptures concerning himself (Luke 24:27).

> For the word of God is alive and active. Sharper than any double-edged sword, it penetrates even to dividing soul and

spirit, joints and marrow; it judges the thoughts and attitudes of the heart (Hebrews 4:12).

1. What do you see as the role of God's Word in the life of a believer?

2. How does recognizing the authority of the Bible as God's Word affirm its right to command your beliefs and your actions?

KEY IDEA

I BELIEVE THE BIBLE IS THE WORD OF GOD AND HAS THE RIGHT TO COMMAND MY BELIEF AND ACTION

We will only give the Bible the right to guide our lives if we believe it is truly from God. This is where we need to begin our discovery. In the Bible itself, we find three main concepts that support the idea that it does, in fact, come directly from God. First, we read that the Bible is *inspired*—or breathed out by God himself. Paul writes that it is "God-breathed" and useful for "teaching, rebuking, correcting, and training in righteousness" (see 2 Timothy 3:16).

Second, we read that God revealed, or breathed, his message into chosen people to be written down. It took forty authors more than 1,400 years to record the sixty-six books we call the Bible. After these inspired works were written, individual books were copied with much scrutiny to ensure authenticity was maintained. In fact, the accuracy rate has been placed at a staggering 99.9 percent! The Bible was then brought to all people when it was translated from the original Hebrew and Greek copies into other languages.

Third, we read that the Bible is infallible, or unfailing, in accomplishing its purposes. What God's Word says will come about, *will* come about. What God's Word says it will do in our lives, it *will* do in our lives (see Isaiah 55:10–11). What we believe about the Bible impacts whether we will let it guide our beliefs and actions. If it is the inspired Word of God, our beliefs will be molded by it. If it is the inspired Word of God, our actions will reflect what we believe.

> *All Scripture is God-breathed and is useful for teaching, rebuking, correcting and training in righteousness, so that the servant of God may be thoroughly equipped for every good work* (2 Timothy 3:16–17).

> *Above all, you must understand that no prophecy of Scripture came about by the prophet's own interpretation of things. For prophecy never had its origin in the human will, but prophets, though human, spoke from God as they were carried along by the Holy Spirit* (2 Peter 1:20–21).

> *"Every word of God is flawless;*
> *he is a shield to those who take refuge in him.*

Do not add to his words,
or he will rebuke you and prove you a liar"
(Proverbs 30:5–6).

1. What do you believe about the reliability of the Bible as God's inspired word to us?

_____

_____

_____

2. Why is it important to believe that the Bible is not only *inspired* but also *infallible*?

_____

_____

_____

KEY APPLICATION
WHAT DIFFERENCE THIS MAKES

If we actually believe the Bible is God's inspired, life-giving, and unfailing Word, how should it affect our lives? First, the Bible should be the lens through which we view the world and everything we encounter. Giving the Bible its rightful place in our lives and submitting to its authority opens our eyes to see the intervention of God in history, in our present lives, and on into the future as he continues to write his grand story.

Second, if we believe the Bible is God's inspired word, we should be motivated to study it to understand God's will. The

Bible forms the content of truth in which we seek to marinate our minds. As our minds are transformed, so are our lives as we trust the Lord to know what is best for us and to guide us (see Proverbs 3:5-6). The Bible is not a book of suggestions. It claims to be the very Word of God and invites us to let it guide every aspect of our lives.

So, are you in or are you out? Do you believe the Bible is the inspired Word of God and has the right to command your beliefs and actions? Will you give it the rightful authority to shape your life?

> *Do not conform to the pattern of this world, but be transformed by the renewing of your mind. Then you will be able to test and approve what God's will is—his good, pleasing and perfect will* (Romans 12:2).

> *Oh, how I love your law!*
> *I meditate on it all day long* (Psalm 119:97).

> *Search me, God, and know my heart;*
> *test me and know my anxious thoughts.*
> *See if there is any offensive way in me,*
> *and lead me in the way everlasting*
> (Psalm 139:23-24).

> *My son, if you accept my words*
> *and store up my commands within you,*
> *turning your ear to wisdom*
> *and applying your heart to understanding—*
> *indeed, if you call out for insight*
> *and cry aloud for understanding,*

and if you look for it as for silver
  and search for it as for hidden treasure,
then you will understand the fear of the LORD
  and find the knowledge of God.
For the LORD gives wisdom;
  from his mouth come knowledge and understanding.
He holds success in store for the upright,
  he is a shield to those whose walk is blameless,
for he guards the course of the just
  and protects the way of his faithful ones
(Proverbs 2:1–8).

1. In what ways have you experienced the Word of God as "alive and active"?

2. How do you see what you believe and what you do being influenced by the Bible?

EVALUATE

As you conclude this personal study, use a scale of 1–6 to rate how strongly you believe the following statements (1 = no belief at all, 6 = complete confidence):

____ I believe the Bible is absolutely true in matters of faith and morals.

____ I believe the words of the Bible are words from God.

____ I believe the Bible has decisive authority over what I say and do.

____ I believe the Bible is relevant to address the needs of contemporary culture.

TAKE ACTION

Memorizing Scripture is a valuable discipline for all believers to exercise. Spend a few minutes each day committing this week's key verse to memory.

KEY VERSE: "All Scripture is God-breathed and is useful for teaching, rebuking, correcting and training in righteousness, so that the servant of God may be thoroughly equipped for every good work" (2 Timothy 3:16–17).

Recite this week's key idea out loud. As you do, ask yourself, *Does my life reflect this statement?*

KEY IDEA: I believe the Bible is the inspired Word of God that guides my beliefs and actions.

Answer the following questions to help you apply this week's key idea to your own life.

1. How would this belief in action express itself in your life?

2. What attributes can be found in someone who knows and is directed by the Bible?

3. If you have reservations about the reliability and/or authority of Scripture, what is your plan for finding answers to your questions?

4. What are some ways you can filter your thoughts and actions through the truth of God's Word?

Session 5

WHO AM I IN CHRIST?

WELCOME

Who am I? Our answer to this question is one of the most important indicators of our happiness and quality of life. If we like our answer to this question, it will prove to be a solid foundation on which to build our lives. If we hate our answer to this question . . . it will not go as well for us. When we open the pages of the Bible, we discover that God has an opinion of who we are in his eyes. He views us as his own beloved children—significant beings, new creations, and heirs to his own kingdom. When we come to see ourselves the same way that God sees us, it leads to a new identity and a new outlook on life. Our worth is no longer defined by what we do but by *who* we know. We are significant because of who we are in Christ.

— VIDEO TEACHING NOTES —

Welcome to session five of *Think Like Jesus*. Spend a few minutes sharing any insights or questions about last week's personal study. Then start the video and use the following outline to record some of the main points. (The answer key is found at the end of the session.)

- **Key Question:** _____ _____ _____?

- **Key Verse:** "Yet to all who did receive him, to those who believed in his name, he gave the right to become _____ of God" (John 1:12).

- **Key Idea:** [I believe] I am _____ because of my _____ as a child of God.

- You are a _____ because you are the child of the ultimate _____.

- **(Key Application #1):** I am free from _____ _____.

- **(Key Application #2):** My worth comes from my position in Christ, not my _____.

- **(Key Application #3):** I live to _____ who I am in Christ, not to _____ who I am.

- **(Key Application #4):** I can focus on _____ others up, not _____ them down.

GETTING STARTED

Begin your discussion by reciting the key verse and key idea together as a group. On your first attempt, use your notes if you need help. On your second attempt, try to state them completely from memory.

KEY VERSE: "Yet to all who did receive him, to those who believed in his name, he gave the right to become children of God" (John 1:12).

KEY IDEA: [I believe] I am significant because of my position as a child of God.

GROUP DISCUSSION

As a group, discuss your thoughts and feelings about the following declarations. Which statements are easy to declare with certainty? Which are more challenging? Why?

- I believe God loves me; therefore, my life has value.
- I believe that I exist to know, love, and serve God.
- I believe God loves me, even when I do not obey him.
- I believe I am forgiven and accepted by God.

Based on your group's dynamics and spiritual maturity, choose the two to three questions that will lead to the best discussion about this week's key idea.

1. Many people find their identity in things that don't last, such as wealth, power, beauty, and influence. Why is it tempting to find your worth in these fading attributes?

2. How has this session given you a better understanding of who you are in God's eyes?

3. How does understanding your identity in Christ change the way you interact with the people in your life?

4. What thoughts, feelings, or experiences, if any, are keeping you from accepting your identity as a child of God?

_____

_____

_____

_____

Read Luke 19:1–9 and choose one to two questions that will lead to the greatest discussion in your group.

1. In what ways did Zacchaeus's conduct change when Jesus restored his identity?

_____

_____

_____

2. If you could "start over" with a new identity as Zacchaeus did, what would you leave in your past?

_____

_____

_____

3. What are some ways your identity in Christ frees you to live without fear or anxiety?

_____

_____

_____

CASE STUDY

Use the following case study as a model for a real-life situation where you might put this week's key idea into practice.

> Sam is one of those guys who appears to be good at everything. He is highly educated, frequently promoted at work, a gourmet cook, and plays the ukulele. He is a model citizen, faithful husband, and coaches his kid's Little League team. But one day you are shocked when Sam's wife asks you to pray for him. She explains that he barely sleeps at night and has been prescribed medication to control his panic attacks. He has always been driven to succeed, she says, but he never seems to find contentment in his achievements.

Using the following key applications from this session, discuss what you could say and do to help Sam find peace in his identity in Christ.

KEY APPLICATION #1: I am free from condemnation.

KEY APPLICATION #2: My worth comes from my position in Christ, not my performance.

KEY APPLICATION #3: I live to express who I am in Christ, not to prove who I am.

KEY APPLICATION #4: I can focus on building others up, not tearing them down.

CLOSING PRAYER

Close your time together with prayer. Share your prayer requests with one another. Ask God to help you put this week's key idea into practice.

FOR NEXT WEEK

Before your next group meeting, be sure to read through the following personal study and complete the exercises.

VIDEO NOTES ANSWER KEY

who am I / children / significant, position / somebody, somebody / condemnation / performance / express, prove / building, tearing

PERSONAL STUDY

Last week you considered your beliefs about the Bible. Perhaps you gained new insights about the importance of the Bible—the Word of God—in your life. Maybe you even gained a new love of Bible reading! Before your next group meeting, complete the following study. Allow the Scripture to take root in your heart as you reflect on who you are as a person.

KEY QUESTION
WHO AM I?

At some point, everyone asks the question, "Who am I?" Some of us like the answer to that question. Some of us do not. And some of us are really not sure about how we would answer that question. If you fall into this last camp, this might help: *God thinks you are significant and even offers you the opportunity to become his beloved child!*

When we accept Jesus as our Lord and Savior, we are given a new identity and a new purpose in life. In the Bible, we find that God's provision through Jesus Christ ushered in a new season of amazing grace that enabled us to have this new identity. This is called the "new covenant" in Scripture because it fulfilled the requirements of the old covenant made with Moses and Abraham. Those who embrace this new covenant and turn from their sins have their sins wiped away. They become a completely new person in God's family.

The beautiful thing about God's kingdom is that all are given access. *All* who welcome Jesus as their Lord are given the opportunity to accept a new identity through him. The story of Zacchaeus, a despised tax collector, shows that even an outcast can be adopted by God and made new (see Luke 19:1–9)! We can move from a position in sin, accept the payment required to release us from its power, and finish with our glorious adoption into God's family.

> *For if, while we were God's enemies, we were reconciled to him through the death of his Son, how much more, having been reconciled, shall we be saved through his life! Not only is this so, but we also boast in God through our Lord Jesus Christ, through whom we have now received reconciliation* (Romans 5:10–11).

> *For we know that our old self was crucified with him so that the body ruled by sin might be done away with, that we should no longer be slaves to sin—because anyone who has died has been set free from sin* (Romans 6:6–7).

> *Yet to all who did receive him, to those who believed in his name, he gave the right to become children of God—children born not of natural descent, nor of human decision or a husband's will, but born of God* (John 1:12–13).

> *See what great love the Father has lavished on us, that we should be called children of God! And that is what we are!* (1 John 3:1).

1. What does God give to those who find their identity in Jesus Christ?

_____

_____

_____

_____

_____

2. How is our identity in Jesus Christ different from our old identity?

_____

_____

_____

_____

_____

KEY IDEA
[I BELIEVE] I AM SIGNIFICANT BECAUSE OF MY POSITION AS A CHILD OF GOD

We need to be mindful of the voices that will come into our lives as we come to understand our new identity in Christ. Sometimes the voices we hear will be echoes from our past—words from an abusive parent, bitter ex-spouse, bullying coach, or even an online comment. Or maybe the voices have never been audible but are scenes in our mind—a picture of a more successful family, an image of missed opportunity, or the reflection in the mirror every morning.

The great news is that when we come to Christ, we no longer have to pay any attention to these voices. God wants to tell us exactly who we are, and the moment we profess our faith in him, we receive a new identity. Each day, God's voice will whisper to us that we are his and silence the voices that have lied to us. As we start to continually listen to God and repeat who we are in him, we can believe his truth and act on it.

Our time on earth is to be spent loving our Father and building his kingdom, which he freely shares with us—now and in eternity. He has given us full access to himself, his character, his gifts, and his qualities. We become his dwelling place because we can take God with us everywhere we go! We are now members of the body of Christ. This great family, led by our Father, gives us a unique sense of eternal purpose and calling.

As citizens of heaven, it doesn't matter where we came from in the past. We now belong to a new kingdom. And as we live here and now, this new identity will help us to impact the world for Christ today and for eternity.

The Spirit himself testifies with our spirit that we are God's children. Now if we are children, then we are heirs—heirs of God and co-heirs with Christ, if indeed we share in his sufferings in order that we may also share in his glory (Romans 8:16–17).

If anyone is in Christ, the new creation has come: The old has gone, the new is here! (2 Corinthians 5:17).

Now you are the body of Christ, and each one of you is a part of it (1 Corinthians 12:27).

1. What are some ways you have been tempted to listen to the voices that attempt to define your identity and purpose in this world?

_____

_____

_____

_____

2. What does God give to those who choose to find their identity in Jesus Christ?

_____

_____

_____

_____

KEY APPLICATION
WHAT DIFFERENCE THIS MAKES

Many people struggle with accepting God's grace and mercy because of things they have done in the past. But the apostle Paul is clear that "there is now no condemnation for those who are in Christ Jesus" (Romans 8:1). This means that past judgment, accusation, and bondage to sin are no more. When another person tries to tell us that we are insignificant or puts us down, we don't have to listen. We know that in Christ, this is simply not true.

Our new identity in Christ also frees us from trying to find our purpose through performance. It is exhausting work to try to prove our worth through our own efforts—a constant rollercoaster of emotions that varies from one day to the next based on whether we feel we are successful or not. Jesus offers us freedom from the tyranny of such demands for approval. He gives us a place at his table and secures our position in him.

As a result of our new identity, we can now focus on building others up instead of tearing them down. As our thinking about who we are changes, it affects our actions... and we begin to reflect the love of God to others. We are set free to use our words to build bridges rather than burn them down, and to use our hands to applaud and not to hurt. As we do this, we will be "Jesus with skin on." We will be an extension of his grace and mercy to the world.

> If anyone acknowledges that Jesus is the Son of God, God lives in them and they in God. And so we know and rely on the love God has for us. God is love. Whoever lives in love lives in God, and God in them. This is how love is made complete among us so that we will have confidence on the day of judgment: In this world we are like Jesus (1 John 4:15–17).

> You are no longer foreigners and strangers, but fellow citizens with God's people and also members of his household, built on the foundation of the apostles and prophets, with Christ Jesus himself as the chief cornerstone. In him the whole building is joined together and rises to become a holy temple in the Lord. And in him you too are being built together to become a dwelling in which God lives by his Spirit (Ephesians 2:19–22).

1. How does your identity in Christ bring freedom to you?

2. What does it look like for a child of God to be "Jesus with skin on" to the world?

EVALUATE

As you conclude this personal study, use a scale of 1–6 to rate how strongly you believe the following statements (1 = no belief at all, 6 = complete confidence):

____ I believe God loves me; therefore, my life has value.

____ I believe that I exist to know, love, and serve God.

____ I believe God loves me, even when I do not obey him.

____ I believe I am forgiven and accepted by God.

TAKE ACTION

Memorizing Scripture is a valuable discipline for all believers to exercise. Spend a few minutes each day committing this week's key verse to memory.

KEY VERSE: "Yet to all who did receive him, to those who believed in his name, he gave the right to become children of God" (John 1:12).

Recite this week's key idea out loud. As you do, ask yourself, *Does my life reflect this statement?*

KEY IDEA: [I believe] I am significant because of my position as a child of God.

Answer the following questions to help you apply this week's key idea to your own life.

1. How would this belief express itself in your life?

_____

_____

_____

_____

2. What visible attributes can be found in those who find their identity in Christ?

_____

_____

_____

_____

_____

3. What behaviors or attitudes would change if you found your value in Christ rather than personal achievements?

_____

_____

_____

_____

_____

4. How can you squash the temptation to prove your significance through performance?

_____

_____

_____

_____

_____

Session 6

WHAT IS THE PURPOSE OF THE CHURCH?

Jesus said to us as his followers, "Whoever believes in me will do the works I have been doing" (John 14:12). What a tall order! But then Christ went even further, saying, "they will do even greater things than these." *Greater works than Jesus?* How is that even possible? On our own, it is certainly *not* possible. However, just like the early followers we read about in the book of Acts, we find that we *can* achieve incredible things for God when we work in cooperation with our brothers and sisters in Christ. Our relationship with God enables us to join together as a body and truly impact the world in a meaningful and fruitful way.

VIDEO TEACHING NOTES

Welcome to session six of *Think Like Jesus*. Spend a few minutes sharing any insights or questions about last week's personal study. Then start the video and use the following outline to record some of the main points. (The answer key is found at the end of the session.)

- **Key Question**: How will God _____ his plan?

- **Key Idea**: I believe the church is God's _____ way to accomplish his _____ on earth today.

- "But you will receive power when the Holy Spirit comes on you; and you will be my _____ in Jerusalem, and in all Judea and Samaria, and to the ends of the earth" (Acts 1:8).

- **Key Verse**: "Instead, speaking the truth in love, we will grow to become in every respect the mature _____ of him who is the head, that is, Christ. From him the whole body, joined and held together by every supporting ligament, grows and builds itself up in love, as each _____ does its work" (Ephesians 4:15–16).

- **(Key Application #1)**: You belong to the body of Christ; don't go looking for _____ in all the wrong places.

- **(Key Application #2)**: God will use the church to _____ his purposes in your life.

- (Key Application #3): God will use _____ to accomplish his purposes in the lives of others and even the world.

GETTING STARTED

Begin your discussion by reciting the key verse and key idea together as a group. On your first attempt, use your notes if you need help. On your second attempt, try to state them completely from memory.

KEY VERSE: "Instead, speaking the truth in love, we will grow to become in every respect the mature body of him who is the head, that is, Christ. From him the whole body, joined and held together by every supporting ligament, grows and builds itself up in love, as each part does its work" (Ephesians 4:15–16).

KEY IDEA: I believe the church is God's primary way to accomplish his purposes on earth.

GROUP DISCUSSION

As a group, discuss your thoughts and feelings about the following declarations. Which statements are easy to declare with certainty? Which are more challenging? Why?

- I believe God gives spiritual gifts to every Christian for service to the church and the community.
- I believe that I cannot grow as a Christian unless I am an active member of a local church.
- I believe the community of true believers is Christ's body on earth.
- I believe the purpose of the church is to share the gospel and nurture Christians to maturity in Christ.

Based on your group's dynamics and spiritual maturity, choose the two to three questions that will lead to the best discussion about this week's key idea.

1. What are some ways your local church has helped you grow in spiritual maturity?

_____

_____

_____

_____

_____

2. If it is unhealthy to live life in isolation, why do so many people choose to live that way?

_____

_____

_____

_____

_____

_____

3. Many people seek to find purpose and community outside of the church. In what ways could this harm the church community and hinder an individual's growth?

_____

_____

_____

_____

_____

4. What are three simple ways that your group could assist your local church in its redemptive mission?

_____

_____

_____

_____

Read Genesis 12:1–3 and choose one to two questions that will lead to the greatest discussion in your group.

1. God's covenantal promise to Abraham and his descendants was to bless them. In turn, they would be a blessing to the world. In what ways are these promises displayed in your church today?

_____

_____

_____

_____

_____

2. What are some ways that you, your family, and your church can be a blessing to the world?

_____

_____

_____

_____

3. How have you personally seen God's blessing on your life?

_____

_____

_____

_____

CASE STUDY

Use the following case study as a model for a real-life situation where you might put this week's key idea into practice.

Your friend Jackie has been a principal at her school for nearly two decades. When you run into her at the grocery store, you can tell that she is not her typical cheerful self. So, you ask if she is okay. Her response catches you off guard. "I'm okay, I guess. This school year has been really tough on me. In fact, each year seems to be more challenging. The kids are great! Don't misunderstand me. I'll never get tired of them.

I just wish I could do more to help. You see, most of my kids come from families that are struggling. The parents have good intentions, but they are ill-equipped financially, relationally, and emotionally—and there is only so much we can do as educators."

Using the following key applications from this session, discuss what advice you would give to Jackie.

KEY APPLICATION #1: You belong to the body of Christ; don't go looking for community in all the wrong places.

KEY APPLICATION #2: God will use the church to accomplish his purposes in your life.

KEY APPLICATION #3: God will use you to accomplish his purposes in the lives of others and even the world.

CLOSING PRAYER

Close your time together with prayer. Share your prayer requests with one another. Ask God to help you put this week's key idea into practice.

FOR NEXT WEEK

Before your next group meeting, be sure to read through the following personal study and complete the exercises.

VIDEO NOTES ANSWER KEY

accomplish / primary, purposes / witnesses / body, part / community / accomplish / you

PERSONAL STUDY

Last week you read about your identity in Christ. Perhaps you learned something new about your place in God's kingdom and how God sees you changed. Before your next group meeting, complete the following study. Allow the Scripture to take root in your heart as you consider how you personally can take part in God's plan for the world.

KEY QUESTION
HOW DOES GOD ACCOMPLISH HIS PURPOSES TODAY?

In the Old Testament, God was in an ongoing relationship with Israel to reveal his name, identity, and plans to the nations. From this single nation would come the solution for all people to come back into a relationship with the one true God. Every account written regarding Israel was intended to point people to the *first* coming of Jesus. But after Christ came into this world and fulfilled his mission to defeat sin and death, God commissioned a new community. This convergence of Jews and Gentiles would form a new family called the church.

The Bible states the church is the *primary*—though not exclusive—method that God uses to accomplish his purposes on earth. Today, a vital mission for this body of believers is to point people toward the second coming of Christ, when he will fully restore God's original vision for his kingdom. At this time, the relationship with God will be restored once and for all.

Those who embrace salvation by grace are inducted and integrated into the church as full members. Although it is true that a person who professes faith in Christ can gain salvation and never become an active member in God's church, this absence of community will create a hindrance not unlike a train with no track or a car with no wheels. The identity may be in place, but there will be no purpose to the existence.

With many other words he warned them; and he pleaded with them, "Save yourselves from this corrupt generation." Those who accepted his message were baptized, and about three thousand were added to their number that day.

They devoted themselves to the apostles' teaching and to fellowship, to the breaking of bread and to prayer. Everyone was filled with awe at the many wonders and signs performed by the apostles. All the believers were together and had everything in common. They sold property and possessions to give to anyone who had need. Every day they continued to meet together in the temple courts. They broke bread in their homes and ate together with glad and sincere hearts, praising God and enjoying the favor of all the people. And the Lord added to their number daily those who were being saved. (Acts 2:40–47).

Instead, speaking the truth in love, we will grow to become in every respect the mature body of him who is the head, that is, Christ (Ephesians 4:15).

Just as a body, though one, has many parts, but all its many parts form one body, so it is with Christ. For we were all baptized by one Spirit so as to form one body—whether Jews or Gentiles, slave or free—and we were all given the one Spirit to drink. Even so the body is not made up of one part but of many (1 Corinthians 12:12–14).

1. How would you describe the body of Christ as God intended it?

2. What do you see as the importance of participating in the church?

KEY IDEA
I BELIEVE THE CHURCH IS GOD'S PRIMARY WAY TO ACCOMPLISH HIS PURPOSES ON EARTH

Jesus commissioned his disciples to spread the good news from Jerusalem and extend his church to all of Judea, and Samaria, and ultimately to the ends of the earth. With the coming of the Holy Spirit, the believers were empowered and shared the gospel boldly. As a result, the church grew in spite of (and often because of) heavy persecution that occurred.

Every belief system is always just one generation away from extinction. So, we must ask how we are doing today in building the body of Christ. Over the past few decades, we've seen a strong trend of young people walking away from the church after they've left their parents' home and their home church. We've also seen many coming back into the fold after "settling down" to family and career. But today we see a new trend—leaving and not coming back.

Certainly, we would all admit the church often doesn't look the way Christ intended it to look. In fact, many people readily confess to not having a problem with *Jesus* as much as with his followers. And then there are those in our fast-paced culture who struggle to be a part of the church because they can't add one more activity to their life list—especially if they no longer see the relevance in the time investment.

However, trends and statistics aside, there are tremendous benefits in being a part of the church—the great community of believers who are daily advancing his kingdom.

"You are the light of the world. A town built on a hill cannot be hidden. Neither do people light a lamp and put it under a bowl. Instead they put it on its stand, and it gives light to everyone in the house. In the same way, let your light shine before others, that they may see your good deeds and glorify your Father in heaven" (Matthew 5:14–16).

Then the church throughout Judea, Galilee and Samaria enjoyed a time of peace and was strengthened. Living in the fear of the Lord and encouraged by the Holy Spirit, it increased in numbers (Acts 9:31).

Now those who had been scattered by the persecution that broke out when Stephen was killed traveled as far as Phoenicia, Cyprus and Antioch, spreading the word only among Jews. Some of them, however, men from Cyprus and Cyrene, went to Antioch and began to speak to Greeks also, telling them the good news about the Lord Jesus. The Lord's hand was with them, and a great number of people believed and turned to the Lord (Acts 11:19–21).

1. How would you define God's mission for the church?

   _____

   _____

   _____

2. How has God used the church to spread the gospel to all people?

   _____

   _____

   _____

   _____

KEY APPLICATION
WHAT DIFFERENCE THIS MAKES

Many people who struggle with church have never been a part of the level of community and relationship that God intended believers to enjoy. They don't understand what is available to them and the benefits that come from being a part of the body of Christ. Perhaps this is because they were part of a community in the past that was not healthy and tore them down. Their experience created an emotional avoidance that is difficult to overcome.

However, when the church functions as God intends, nothing else on earth works quite like it. Christ's bride is not an *organization* but an *organism*. It's not so much about the type of programs that the church offers but the health of its people. The true church is not a *building* but a *body*. When functioning properly, it is a family that serves to surround people with strength and grace, while continually pointing them toward the abundant life in Christ.

Certainly, we can grow spiritually on our own, but when we get in step with a body of believers, it can accelerate our growth through *accountability* and *synergy*. Accountability simply means everyone in the group has each other's back and everyone is encouraged to grow and mature. Synergy means the cohesion of the group is a greater force than the individual sum of its members. Together, believers who operate in the body of Christ—the church—produce an overall better result than each person working alone toward the same goal.

In the body of Christ, we become a part of a movement that is larger than ourselves. This truth should serve as a powerful motivator for us to be involved in ministry, for when we see ourselves as part of a far larger plan and purpose, we will become infused with the power of eternity. We can indeed accomplish those "greater things" to which Christ referred.

Two are better than one,
because they have a good return for their labor:

If either of them falls down,
    one can help the other up.
But pity anyone who falls
    and has no one to help them up
(Ecclesiastes 4:9–10).

I consider my life worth nothing to me; my only aim is to finish the race and complete the task the Lord Jesus has given me—the task of testifying to the good news of God's grace (Acts 20:24).

Very truly I tell you, whoever believes in me will do the works I have been doing, and they will do even greater things than these, because I am going to the Father. And I will do whatever you ask in my name, so that the Father may be glorified in the Son. You may ask me for anything in my name, and I will do it (John 14:12–14).

1. What happens when believers in Christ work together for God's purposes?

_____

_____

_____

2. How have you seen the church promote accountability and synergy in its members?

_____

_____

_____

EVALUATE

As you conclude this personal study, use a scale of 1–6 to rate how strongly you believe the following statements (1 = no belief at all, 6 = complete confidence):

_____ I believe God gives spiritual gifts to every Christian for service to the church and the community.

_____ I believe that I cannot grow as a Christian unless I am an active member of a local church.

_____ I believe the community of true believers is Christ's body on earth.

_____ I believe the purpose of the church is to share the gospel and nurture Christians to maturity in Christ.

TAKE ACTION

Memorizing Scripture is a valuable discipline for all believers to exercise. Spend a few minutes each day committing this week's key verse to memory.

KEY VERSE: "Instead, speaking the truth in love, we will grow to become in every respect the mature body of him who is the head, that is, Christ. From him the whole body, joined and held together by every supporting ligament, grows and builds itself up in love, as each part does its work" (Ephesians 4:15–16).

Recite this week's key idea out loud. As you do, ask yourself, *Does my life reflect this statement?*

> **KEY IDEA:** I believe the church is God's primary way to accomplish his purposes on earth.

Answer the following questions to help you apply this week's key idea to your own life.

1. What behaviors help you recognize someone who believes the church is God's primary way to accomplish his purposes on earth?

_____

_____

_____

_____

_____

2. What, if anything, hinders you from fully offering your time and abilities to the mission of the church?

_____

_____

_____

_____

_____

3. What is something you can do this week to demonstrate
   your belief in the church as God's primary way to accomplish his purposes on earth?

   _____

   _____

   _____

   _____

   _____

   _____

Session 7

HOW DOES GOD VALUE PEOPLE?

It's easy to become desensitized when we listen to the daily news. The massive problems in this world—poverty, disease, natural disasters, economic crises, violence—make it seem as though some kind of evil is destined for each day's headlines. But for believers in Christ, the issue is not what *problem* in the world can we solve but what Jesus would have us to do for the *people* who are being affected by all these crises. Simply determining to be humanitarian is a noble goal, but joining God in his work is the best labor of love we can offer. Jesus himself is our goal and purpose—the work is simply the result of what we do as we walk in step with him.

VIDEO TEACHING NOTES

Welcome to session seven of *Think Like Jesus*. Spend a few minutes sharing any insights or questions about last week's personal study. Then start the video and use the following outline to record some of the main points. (The answer key is found at the end of the session.)

- **Key Question:** How does God _____ people?

- **Key Idea:** I believe _____ people are loved by God and _____ Jesus Christ as their Savior.

- "We all, like sheep, have gone astray, each of us has turned to our own _____" (Isaiah 53:6).

- **Key Verse:** "For God so loved the world that he _____ his one and only Son, that whoever believes in him shall not _____ but have eternal life" (John 3:16).

- "But God demonstrates his own love for us in this: While we were still _____, Christ died for us" (Romans 5:8).

- (Key Application #1): I value _____ human life.

- (Key Application #2): I see and treat all people the way _____ sees and treats them.

- (Key Application #3): I am compelled to tell all people about _____.

GETTING STARTED

Begin your discussion by reciting the key verse and key idea together as a group. On your first attempt, use your notes if you need help. On your second attempt, try to state them completely from memory.

KEY VERSE: "For God so loved the world that he gave his one and only Son, that whoever believes in him shall not perish but have eternal life" (John 3:16).

KEY IDEA: I believe all people are loved by God and need Jesus Christ as their Savior.

GROUP DISCUSSION

As a group, discuss your thoughts and feelings about the following declarations. Which statements are easy to declare with certainty? Which are more challenging? Why?

- I believe that each person possesses a sinful nature and is in need of God's forgiveness.

- I believe we are created in the image of God and therefore have equal value, regardless of race, religion, or gender.
- I believe all people are loved by God; therefore, I too should love them.
- I believe God desires all people to have a relationship with Jesus Christ.

Based on your group's dynamics and spiritual maturity, choose the two to three questions that will lead to the best discussion about this week's key idea.

1. What thoughts and feelings come to mind when you consider God's radical love for you and the people of this world?

2. Do you find it difficult to receive God's love and forgiveness? Why or why not?

3. What personal disciplines can you adopt that would invite the Holy Spirit to change your heart toward difficult people?

4. Think of a time when God changed your heart toward a person or people group. What specifically caused the change within you?

Read Romans 1:18–32 and Luke 6:27–36 and choose one to two questions that will lead to the greatest discussion in your group.

1. What does Paul reveal in Romans 1:18–32 about humanity and the human condition?

2. How does loving your enemies show the world that you are a child of God?

_____

_____

_____

_____

_____

3. The Bible calls you to love difficult people the way God does. Is this possible? If so, how?

_____

_____

_____

_____

CASE STUDY

Use the following case study as a model for a real-life situation where you might put this week's key idea into practice.

Charlie, Jamie, and their two kids have been coming to church with you for the last year and a half. In the beginning they were reluctant, but now they are eagerly seeking to apply God's Word to their lives—and the changes are evident. During a lunch conversation, Charlie mentions a neighbor who has been getting on his nerves. "Honestly, I'm reluctant to say it, but I can't stand the guy. His yard is always a mess, he never makes eye contact, and we couldn't be farther apart when it comes to politics. During election times, his yard is filled with signs supporting people and ideas that I think are just plain dangerous. I know we are supposed to love our neighbors as ourselves, but I'm having a hard time finding something lovable about this guy."

Using the following key applications from this session, discuss what practical advice you would give to Charlie.

KEY APPLICATION #1: I value all human life.

KEY APPLICATION #2: I see and treat all people the way God sees and treats them.

KEY APPLICATION #3: I am compelled to tell all people about Jesus.

CLOSING PRAYER

Close your time together with prayer. Share your prayer requests with one another. Ask God to help you put this week's key idea into practice.

FOR NEXT WEEK

Before your next group meeting, be sure to read through the following personal study and complete the exercises.

VIDEO NOTES ANSWER KEY

see / all, need / way / gave, perish / sinners / all / God / Jesus

PERSONAL STUDY

Last week you took a deeper look at the role of the church in God's great plan. Perhaps you discovered the part you personally play in that plan. Before your next group meeting, complete the following study. Allow the Scripture to take root in your heart and ask that God would reveal to you why it's easier for you to love some people and groups than others.

KEY QUESTION
HOW DOES GOD SEE PEOPLE?

God created everything, but the pinnacle of creation was human beings—creatures crafted in his own image. Humanity is special, and the Bible is the record of that love story between God and humans. From the beginning of time to the era of the modern-day church, God has loved and pursued his people in order to restore his image within and among them.

The Bible clearly reveals that God loves all people the same (see John 3:16). He loves the one in prison who committed heinous crimes as much as he does the faithful Sunday school teacher. He loves the tiny child struggling to survive in the desert of the Sudan as much as the Hollywood celebrity living in luxury. God sees all, hears all, and loves all.

As the apostle Paul worked diligently to establish and sustain churches, his calling from God was always crystal clear—to reach out to *all* people. As the old adage goes, "The ground is level at the foot of the cross." Someday, God will deal with the godless and the wicked (see Romans 1:14–20). This is exactly why *all* people need to be saved—and exactly why each of us, as members of the body of Christ, need to be reaching the world with the gospel.

> *For God so loved the world that he gave his one and only Son, that whoever believes in him shall not perish but have eternal life* (John 3:16).

> *He is the one we proclaim, admonishing and teaching everyone with all wisdom, so that we may present everyone fully mature in Christ. To this end I strenuously contend with all the energy Christ so powerfully works in me* (Colossians 1:28–29).

> *For I am not ashamed of the gospel, because it is the power of God that brings salvation to everyone who believes: first to the Jew, then to the Gentile. For in the gospel the righteousness of God is revealed—a righteousness that is by faith from first to last, just as it is written: "The righteous will live by faith." The wrath of God is being revealed from heaven against all the godlessness and wickedness of people, who suppress the truth by their wickedness, since what may be known about God is plain to them, because God has made it plain to them. For since the creation of the world God's invisible qualities—his eternal power and divine nature—have been clearly seen, being understood from what has been made, so that people are without excuse* (Romans 1:16–20).

1. What is God's desire for the people he created?

   _____

   _____

   _____

   _____

2. What problems in our world challenge the fulfillment of
   what God desires for humanity?

   _____

   _____

   _____

   _____

KEY IDEA

I BELIEVE ALL PEOPLE ARE LOVED BY GOD AND NEED JESUS CHRIST AS THEIR SAVIOR

God is the origin of all life. He created the cosmos and everything in it. He created the earth so he could be with the people he created. Unfortunately, the first two people—Adam
and Eve—rejected God's vision for his creation, causing sin to
enter into their nature and thereby making them unfit for
community with a holy God. The greatest pandemic ever experienced by humanity is the transference of this "sin DNA"
to every generation.

Despite the sin that has permeated his creation, God remains faithful to his people. God's love for us is unending
and undeserved . . . and he desires to save *everyone*. To this

end, God has brought us—as his followers—into the family business of placing the needs of others first and changing the future of anyone who responds to the message of salvation. In God's kingdom, even helping a person with a temporary necessity has an eternal purpose.

Jesus made our mission abundantly clear in meeting the needs of the forgotten, the unlovely, and the unpopular. His declaration that to serve them is to serve him is both counter-cultural and life-changing (see Matthew 25:34–40). It is also clear that he desires for us to share the message of salvation with the world (see Mark 16:15). *All* have sinned, and *all* are in need of salvation. *All* are offered salvation . . . but it is our role to share that news with a hurting world.

> *Dear friends, although I was very eager to write to you about the salvation we share, I felt compelled to write and urge you to contend for the faith that was once for all entrusted to God's holy people. For certain individuals whose condemnation was written about long ago have secretly slipped in among you. They are ungodly people, who pervert the grace of our God into a license for immorality and deny Jesus Christ our only Sovereign and Lord* (Jude 3–4).

> *In him was life, and that life was the light of all mankind. The light shines in the darkness, and the darkness has not overcome it (John 1:4–5).*

> *The Father loves the Son and has placed everything in his hands. Whoever believes in the Son has eternal life, but whoever rejects the Son will not see life, for God's wrath remains on them* (John 3:35–36).

1. How would you describe God's original intent for the human race?

_____

_____

_____

_____

2. Why is the provision of salvation through Jesus such a great gift?

_____

_____

_____

_____

KEY APPLICATION
WHAT DIFFERENCE THIS MAKES

How would life change if we started to see people as God sees them? How would the world change if we truly believed the only way for people to enter heaven is through Christ? First, we would place a value on all human life. We would come to realize each person is formed and knit together by God in the womb of their mother (see Psalm 139:13). The youngest or oldest person in the world has not diminished in value one ounce in God's eyes or in ours.

Second, seeing people through God's eyes would change the way we treat them. Our human tendency to place different values on people is inconsistent with God's design. When we show equal value to the broken, bruised, and abandoned in our society, God takes note and rewards us. Authentic behavior flows from a heart of genuine belief in human value.

Third, seeing people through God's eyes compels us to tell all people about the love of Christ. We can share the hope we have in Jesus anytime, anyplace, to anyone. By sharing the gospel with all people, wherever we go, we have the opportunity to change the world by changing people's hearts. This will change families for generations to come . . . and it will change us. We will become more loving people as we learn to value all people.

If God has his way in our minds and hearts through our obedience, we can accomplish these things. We can change the lives of those in our circle of influence by sharing our story of salvation and redemption. But it will require us to first reach out.

So in Christ Jesus you are all children of God through faith, for all of you who were baptized into Christ have clothed yourselves with Christ. There is neither Jew nor Gentile, neither slave nor free, nor is there male and female, for you are all one in Christ Jesus (Galatians 3:26–28).

But in your hearts revere Christ as Lord. Always be prepared to give an answer to everyone who asks you to give the reason for the hope that you have (1 Peter 3:15).

How, then, can they call on the one they have not believed in? And how can they believe in the one of whom they have not heard? And how can they hear without someone preaching to them? And how can anyone preach unless they are sent?

As it is written: "How beautiful are the feet of those who bring good news!" (Romans 10:14–15).

1. What is God's goal for the people he puts in your life?

_____

_____

_____

_____

2. What answer would you give to someone who asks you about your hope in Christ?

_____

_____

_____

_____

_____

TAKE ACTION

As you conclude this personal study, use a scale of 1–6 to rate how strongly you believe the following statements (1 = no belief at all, 6 = complete confidence):

_____ I believe that each person possesses a sinful nature and is in need of God's forgiveness.

_____ I believe we are created in the image of God and therefore have equal value, regardless of race, religion, or gender.

    I believe all people are loved by God; therefore, I too should love them.

    I believe God desires all people to have a relationship with Jesus Christ.

TAKE ACTION

Memorizing Scripture is a valuable discipline for all believers to exercise. Spend a few minutes each day committing this week's key verse to memory.

KEY VERSE: "For God so loved the world that he gave his one and only Son, that whoever believes in him shall not perish but have eternal life" (John 3:16).

Recite this week's key idea out loud. As you do, ask yourself, *Does my life reflect this statement?*

KEY IDEA: I believe all people are loved by God and need Jesus Christ as their Savior.

Answer the following questions to help you apply this week's key idea to your own life.

1. What behaviors help you recognize someone who believes all people are loved by God and need Jesus Christ as their Savior?

_____

_____

_____

_____

_____

2. What, if anything, hinders you from fully loving people the way God loves them?

_____

_____

_____

_____

_____

3. What is something you can do this week to demonstrate this belief?

_____

_____

_____

_____

_____

Session 8

WHAT IS ETERNITY GOING TO BE LIKE?

Blaise Pascal was an inventor, mathematician, physicist, and theological writer who lived in the 1600s. At one point, as science and theology collided in his heart, he came to the conclusion that all of us must make a wager about what we believe. On the one hand, we can believe that God exists, loves us, and has prepared a place for those who follow and obey him when this life is over. On the other hand, we can believe there is no God and that this life . . . is all there is for us. For Pascal, believing in God led to a happier existence, and the consequences for being wrong in his belief was much less severe than the alternative. Yet still, each of us must make our own wager. Will we wager that the Bible's promises are true—and choose to live in light of eternity?

VIDEO TEACHING NOTES

Welcome to session eight of *Think Like Jesus*. Spend a few minutes sharing any insights or questions about last week's personal study. Then start the video and use the following outline to record some of the main points. (The answer key is found at the end of the session.)

- **Key Question:** What happens _____?

- **Key Idea:** I believe there is a heaven and a hell and that Jesus will return to judge all people and to establish his _____ kingdom.

- "Suddenly a chariot of fire and horses of fire appeared and separated the two of them, and Elijah went up to _____ in a whirlwind" (2 Kings 2:11).

- When our body exhales its final breath, our spirit exits the body and goes to one of two places— _____ or _____.

- **Key Verse:** "Do not let your hearts be troubled. You believe in God; believe also in me. My Father's house has many rooms; if that were not so, would I have told you that I am going there to prepare a _____ for you?" (John 14:1–2).

- **(Key Application #1):** Live with _____ every day, regardless of the circumstances around us.

- **(Key Application #2):** Love people with freedom and boldness, because our future is _____ in him.

- **(Key Application #3):** Lead more people into a relationship with Christ, because we want to _____ this great hope with others.

GETTING STARTED

Begin your discussion by reciting the key verse and key idea together as a group. On your first attempt, use your notes if you need help. On your second attempt, try to state them completely from memory.

KEY VERSE: "Do not let your hearts be troubled. You believe in God; believe also in me. My Father's house has many rooms; if that were not so, would I have told you that I am going there to prepare a place for you?" (John 14:1–2).

KEY IDEA: I believe there is a heaven and a hell and that Jesus will return to judge all people and to establish his eternal kingdom.

GROUP DISCUSSION

As a group, discuss your thoughts and feelings about the following declarations. Which statements are easy to declare with certainty? Which are more challenging? Why?

- I believe it is important to share the gospel with my neighbor because Christ has commanded me to do so.
- I believe that people who deliberately reject Jesus Christ as Savior will not inherit eternal life.
- I believe that every person is subject to the judgment of God.
- I believe all people who place their trust in Jesus Christ will spend eternity in heaven.

Based on your group's dynamics and spiritual maturity, choose the two to three questions that will lead to the best discussion about this week's key idea.

1. How would you describe the moment you became aware of your mortality and pondered what would happen after your death?

2. What is it about heaven that brings you hope? What about it is uncertain? What about it brings you freedom?

3. What is it about the life, death, and resurrection of Jesus that led you to put your faith in him?

4. How does having a secured future in heaven affect the way you live your life in the present?

Read 1 Corinthians 15:1–28 and 35–58 and choose one to two questions that will lead to the greatest discussion in your group.

1. In these passages, Paul is refuting the teachings of other religious leaders in Corinth who claimed there was no resurrection of the dead. In what ways does this belief he was combating clash with the gospel of Jesus Christ?

2. Our belief in eternity gives us hope. How would this change if there were no resurrection of the dead?

3. Why do you think Paul refers to Christians who have died as "those that have fallen asleep"? How does this reflect his belief in eternity?

_____

_____

_____

_____

CASE STUDY

Use the following case study as a model for a real-life situation where you might put this week's key idea into practice.

> Your neighbor's brother was tragically killed in a recent car accident. Rhonda has always been a great neighbor and good friend. In order to show your condolences, you stop by her house with sympathetic words and a bouquet of flowers. You've never discussed religion before, but this accident has shaken her up. She asks you, "What do you think happens after we die?"

Using the following key applications from this session, discuss how you would answer Rhonda's question.

KEY APPLICATION #1: Live with hope every day, regardless of the circumstances around us.

KEY APPLICATION #2: Love people with freedom and boldness, because our future is secure in him.

KEY APPLICATION #3: Lead more people into a relationship with Christ, because we want to share this great hope with others.

CLOSING PRAYER

Close your time together with prayer. Share your prayer requests with one another. Ask God to help you put this week's key idea into practice.

FOR NEXT WEEK

Be sure to read through the following personal study and complete the exercises.

VIDEO NOTES ANSWER KEY

next / eternal / heaven / heaven, hell / place / hope / secure / share

PERSONAL STUDY

Last week you explored your beliefs about humanity. Perhaps you learned something about yourself or about God that will help you see others in the way Jesus sees them. Before your next group meeting, complete the following study. Allow the Scripture to take root in your heart as you consider your own beliefs about the future life that is to come.

KEY QUESTION
WHAT HAPPENS NEXT?

Throughout the ages, people have gambled with the question of eternity—about whether God exists and what this means for their future after death. This gamble is where science and faith often collide. Does belief in God—and the hope of a life after this world—make rational sense? Does believing provide a potentially happier life than not believing?

While non-Christians may struggle with these questions, believers in Christ see through this dilemma of the soul. The confidence we have in the security of our future home allows us to spend our time building God's kingdom *now* as we *look forward* to the time when we will be in heaven with God. What awaits us on the other side gives us hope and motivation for today, for we know that while our earthly bodies will go into the grave, our spirit will live on.

The grand promise of God—and the ultimate hope for all Christians—is the resurrection. Just as Christ was raised from the dead and received an imperishable body, so will all those who believe in Christ. The Bible reveals that the event that will trigger this promised resurrection is the second coming of Christ. For this reason, we can echo and agree with the words of the disciple John: "Amen. Come, Lord Jesus" (Revelation 22:20).

> "Do not let your hearts be troubled. You believe in God; believe also in me. My Father's house has many rooms; if that were not so, would I have told you that I am going there to prepare a place for you? And if I go and prepare a place for you, I will come back and take you to be with me that you also may be where I am" (John 14:1–3).

> Christ has indeed been raised from the dead, the firstfruits of those who have fallen asleep. For since death came through a man, the resurrection of the dead comes also through a man. For as in Adam all die, so in Christ all will be made alive (1 Corinthians 15:20–22).

> The sting of death is sin, and the power of sin is the law. But thanks be to God! He gives us the victory through our Lord Jesus Christ. Therefore, my dear brothers and sisters, stand firm. Let nothing move you. Always give yourselves fully to the work of the Lord, because you know that your labor in the Lord is not in vain (1 Corinthians 15:56–58).

1. How does what the Bible says about heaven and hell compare with some of our culture's popular notions of what happens after we die?

_____

_____

_____

_____

2. What hope do you have for the future? What is the role of belief in Christ in this hope?

_____

_____

_____

_____

KEY IDEA

I BELIEVE THERE IS A HEAVEN AND A HELL AND THAT JESUS WILL RETURN TO ESTABLISH HIS ETERNAL KINGDOM

We don't like the truth about hell, but it is a part of the gospel message. We have to take God's Word as a whole and accept even the areas we don't like or wish were not there. Of course, those who have received Christ's offer of salvation by grace no longer need to be concerned about this matter anyway, because he has removed this fear from our future.

The Bible states that Jesus is going to return to the earth, and his first order of business will be to judge humankind.

When Jesus returns, he will make all things right, and everything will come under the authority of his justice. He will throw Satan and his followers, along with sin and death, into the lake of fire. His followers will then receive an imperishable, resurrected body, just as Christ has. Jesus and his people will then reside on a new earth surrounded by a new heaven. For the Christian, this is the future. When we say, "the best is yet to come," we can confidently mean what we say! On this great day, God himself will live among us.

There are varied beliefs about the details leading up to this momentous occasion, but all followers of Jesus embrace its truth and significance. Often, the Bible refers to the return of Christ as the "day of the Lord." On that great day, God will resurrect the faithful who have already died and bring them together with the believers who are remaining on earth. All will receive resurrected bodies, and we will be with the Lord Jesus forever!

Then I saw a great white throne and him who was seated on it. The earth and the heavens fled from his presence, and there was no place for them. And I saw the dead, great and small, standing before the throne, and books were opened. Another book was opened, which is the book of life. The dead were judged according to what they had done as recorded in the books. . . . Then death and Hades were thrown into the lake of fire. The lake of fire is the second death. Anyone whose name was not found written in the book of life was thrown into the lake of fire (Revelation 20:11-12, 14-15).

Listen, I tell you a mystery: We will not all sleep, but we will all be changed—in a flash, in the twinkling of an eye, at the last trumpet. For the trumpet will sound, the dead will be raised imperishable, and we will be changed (1 Corinthians 15:51–52).

According to the Lord's word, we tell you that we who are still alive, who are left until the coming of the Lord, will certainly not precede those who have fallen asleep. For the Lord himself will come down from heaven, with a loud command, with the voice of the archangel and with the trumpet call of God, and the dead in Christ will rise first. After that, we who are still alive and are left will be caught up together with them in the clouds to meet the Lord in the air. And so we will be with the Lord forever. Therefore encourage one another with these words (1 Thessalonians 4:15–18).

1. Why is it important to respond to God's invitation for salvation and eternal life?

_____

_____

_____

_____

2. Why do you think some people don't accept God's gift of salvation and eternal life?

_____

_____

_____

_____

KEY APPLICATION
WHAT DIFFERENCE THIS MAKES

If we truly believe God has prepared an eternal home for us, then we can live with hope every day, regardless of the circumstances around us. We can also love people with freedom and boldness because we know that our future is secure. As we love others, we can share our great hope with them and lead them into a relationship with Christ.

Sharing the hope that you have found in Christ should truly be a life-or-death endeavor. Just consider the people in your life who have not accepted Jesus as their Lord and Savior. Does their eternal future impact your desire to show them God's love and salvation? Evaluate the opportunities you have ahead to boldly, lovingly, and freely share the gospel with them.

If your life has an absence of non-Christians, consider how you can gain a hunger and a drive to see others come to faith in Christ. If you are surrounded by non-Christians, be encouraged that God is working on your behalf to use your every word and action to bring those people to him. Keep praying, be inspired, and never give up. Imagine, one day, each person giving a testimony of how you introduced him or her to freedom into eternity. Know that you are a part of the salvation process—and God will use you as you submit to him.

> So then, dear friends, since you are looking forward to this, make every effort to be found spotless, blameless and at peace with him. Bear in mind that our Lord's patience means salvation (2 Peter 3:14–15).

What, after all, is Apollos? And what is Paul? Only servants, through whom you came to believe—as the Lord has assigned to each his task. I planted the seed, Apollos watered it, but God has been making it grow. So neither the one who plants nor the one who waters is anything, but only God, who makes things grow. The one who plants and the one who waters have one purpose, and they will each be rewarded according to their own labor (1 Corinthians 3:5–8).

You, dear friends, by building yourselves up in your most holy faith and praying in the Holy Spirit, keep yourselves in God's love as you wait for the mercy of our Lord Jesus Christ to bring you to eternal life (Jude 20–21).

1. How are you encouraged to live your life today considering Christ's imminent return?

2. Who in your life needs salvation and hope in Christ?

EVALUATE

As you conclude this personal study, use a scale of 1–6 to rate how strongly you believe the following statements (1 = no belief at all, 6 = complete confidence):

____ I believe it is important to share the gospel with my neighbor because Christ has commanded me to do so.

____ I believe that people who deliberately reject Jesus Christ as Savior will not inherit eternal life.

____ I believe that every person is subject to the judgment of God.

____ I believe all people who place their trust in Jesus Christ will spend eternity in heaven.

TAKE ACTION

Memorizing Scripture is a valuable discipline for all believers to exercise. Spend a few minutes each day committing this week's key verse to memory.

KEY VERSE: "Do not let your hearts be troubled. You believe in God; believe also in me. My Father's house has many rooms; if that were not so, would I have told you that I am going there to prepare a place for you?" (John 14:1–2).

Recite this week's key idea out loud. As you do, ask yourself, *Does my life reflect this statement?*

> **KEY IDEA:** I believe there is a heaven and a hell and that Jesus will return to judge all people and to establish his eternal kingdom.

Answer the following questions to help you apply this week's key idea to your own life.

1. What behaviors help you recognize someone who believes Jesus will return to judge all people and to establish his eternal kingdom?

2. What, if anything, hinders you from believing in the afterlife?

3. What is something you can do this week to demonstrate this belief?

_____

_____

_____

_____

_____

_____

LEADER'S GUIDE

Thank you for your willingness to lead your group through this study! What you have chosen to do is valuable and will make a great difference in the lives of others. The rewards of being a leader are different from those of participating, and we hope that as you lead you will find your own walk with Jesus deepened by this experience.

Think Like Jesus is an eight-session study built around video content and small-group interaction. As the group leader, just think of yourself as the host of a dinner party. Your job is to take care of your guests by managing all the behind-the-scenes details so that when everyone arrives, they can just enjoy time together.

As the group leader, your role is not to answer all the questions or reteach the content—the video and study guide will do most of that work. Your job is to guide the experience and cultivate your small group into a kind of teaching community. This will make it a place for members to process, question, and reflect—not receive more instruction.

Before your first meeting, make sure everyone in the group gets a copy of the study guide. This will keep everyone on the same page and help the process run more smoothly. If some group members are unable to purchase the guide, arrange it so that people can share the resource with other group members. Giving everyone access to all the material will position this study to be as rewarding an experience as possible. Everyone should feel free to write in his or her study guide and bring it to group every week.

SETTING UP THE GROUP

You will need to determine with your small group how long you want to meet each week so that you can plan your time accordingly. Generally, most groups like to meet for either ninety minutes or two hours, so you could use one of the following schedules:

SECTION	90 MINUTES	120 MINUTES
WELCOME (members arrive and get settled)	10 minutes	15 minutes
WATCH (watch the teaching material together and take notes)	15 minutes	15 minutes
DISCUSS (recite the key verse and key idea and discuss the study questions you selected)	40 minutes	60 minutes
CASE STUDY (go through the case study using the key applications for the session)	15 minutes	20 minutes
PRAY (close your time in prayer)	10 minutes	10 minutes

As the group leader, you will want to create an environment that encourages sharing and learning. A church sanctuary or formal classroom may not be as ideal as a living room in this regard, because those locations can feel formal and less intimate. No matter what setting you choose, provide enough comfortable seating for everyone, and, if possible, arrange the seats in a semicircle so everyone can see the video easily. This will make transition between the video and group conversation more efficient and natural.

Try to get to the meeting site early so you can greet participants as they arrive. Simple refreshments create a welcoming atmosphere and can be a wonderful addition to a group study evening. Try to take food and pet allergies into account to make your guests as comfortable as possible. You may also want to consider offering childcare to couples with children who want to attend. Finally, be sure your media technology is working properly. Managing these details up front will make the rest of your group experience flow smoothly and provide a welcoming space to engage the content of *Think Like Jesus*.

STRUCTURING THE GROUP TIME

Once everyone has arrived, it's time to begin the group. Here are some simple tips to make your group time healthy, enjoyable, and effective.

First, begin the meeting with a short prayer and remind the group members to put their phones on silent. This is a way to make sure you can all be present with one another and with God. Next, watch the video and instruct the participants to follow along in their guides and take notes. After the video teaching, have the group recite the key verse and key idea together before moving on to the discussion questions.

Encourage all the group members to participate in the discussion, but make sure they know they don't have to do so. As the discussion progresses, you may want to follow up with comments such as, "Tell me more about that," or, "Why did you answer that way?" This will allow the group participants to deepen their reflections and invite meaningful sharing in a nonthreatening way.

Note that you have been given multiple questions to use in each session, and you do not have to use them all or even follow them in order. Feel free to pick and choose questions based on either the needs of your group or how the conversation is flowing. Also, don't be afraid of silence. Offering a question and allowing up to thirty seconds of silence is okay. It allows people space to think about how they want to respond and also gives them time to do so.

As group leader, you are the boundary keeper for your group. Do not let anyone (yourself included) dominate the group time. Keep an eye out for group members who might be tempted to "attack" folks they disagree with or try to "fix" those having struggles. These kinds of behaviors can derail a group's momentum, so they need to be steered in a different direction. Model active listening and encourage everyone in your group to do the same. This will make your group time a safe space and create a positive community.

CONCLUDING THE GROUP TIME

Each session in *Think Like Jesus* ends with a case study to help the group members process the key concepts and apply them to a real-life situation. At the conclusion of session one, invite the group members to complete the between-sessions personal studies for that week. Explain that you will be providing some time before the video teaching next week for anyone to share insights. (Do this as part of the opening "Welcome" beginning in session two, right before you watch the video.) Let them know sharing is optional.

Thank you again for taking the time to lead your group and helping them to understand what it means to *Think Like Jesus*. You are making a difference in the lives of others and having an impact for the kingdom of God!

If You Want to Grow in Your Faith, You Must Engage God's Word

What you believe in your heart will define who you become. God wants you to become like Jesus—it is the most truthful and powerful way to live—and the journey to becoming like Jesus begins by thinking like Jesus.

Jesus compared the Christian life to a vine. He is the vine; you are the branches. If you remain in the vine of Christ, over time you will produce amazing and scrumptious fruit for all to see and taste. You begin to act like Jesus, and become more like Jesus.

In the **Believe Bible Study Series**, bestselling author and pastor Randy Frazee helps you ask three big questions:

- What do I believe and why does it matter?
- How can I put my faith into action?
- Am I becoming the person God wants me to be?

Each of the three eight-session studies in this series include video teaching from Randy Frazee and a study guide with video study notes, group discussion questions, Scripture reading, and activities for personal growth and reflection.

As you journey through this study series, whether in a group or on your own, one simple truth will become undeniably clear: what you believe drives everything.

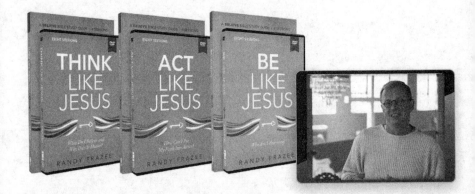

Available now at your favorite bookstore, or streaming video on StudyGateway.com.

— ALSO AVAILABLE —

Dive Deeper Into God's Word

Believe is a unique Bible reader that helps Christians understand what the Bible says about our beliefs, actions, and character. This topical, abridged Bible illuminates the core beliefs of the Christian faith to help you think, act, and be more like Christ.

A helpful companion to the Believe Bible Study Series, *Believe* includes 30 days of Scripture prayerfully selected by Pastor Randy Frazee that expand on and accompany the big ideas in this study series.

Each chapter uses short topical passages from the most read, most trusted New International Version (NIV) to help you live the story of the Bible. As you journey through this Bible, whether in a group or on your own, one simple truth will become undeniably clear: what you believe drives everything.

Experience the lasting transformation that comes from knowing what you believe, understanding in your heart why it matters, and living like Jesus calls you to live.

You know the story. Now live the story. Believe.

Hardcover
9780310443834

Available now at your favorite bookstore.